Mind Power for Musicians

Mental techniques for improving musical skill.

Doug Oliver

Contents

1
Introduction

I'VE ALWAYS BEEN fascinated by the science of sports psychology and the fact that athletic performance can be improved with the use of mental conditioning. Most people are aware of how one can improve a physical activity by getting psyched ("Be the ball" ... remember that one). Then one day it dawned on me. Why not apply the principles of sports psychology to my musicianship rather than just focusing on scales, chords, or playing technique? What if I were to work on applying aspects of mind control that would directly affect my overall musical ability?

The first thing I had to deal with was my poor memory. There would be times I would forget the arrangements of songs and other times I would have trouble remembering chord or scale structures. I read up on various ways to exercise the mind's ability to memorize information and started learning techniques for improving memory. I was amazed to learn that memory, like any skill, can be improved upon. After applying what I learned, I soon noticed a significant improvement.

With the improvements clearly noticeable I broadened my search to the area of stage fright. At that point in my musical career, I was focusing on composing and recording songs in my home studio, so I wasn't playing on stage as often as I had before. But even occasional jam sessions reminded me of how fear and self-consciousness could reduce my playing ability by half if not more. I knew I had to overcome stage fright if I ever wanted to put a band together to perform my original music.

I then realized there were many other ways I could improve my musical abilities by focusing on specific aspects of my mind. After all, without the mind, there is no music (obvious enough), so it stands to reason that the stronger the mind, the better you are as a musician. It was then that I decided to record and organize my research into a book. This began a four-year process that led to the reading of over forty books, countless websites, and other sources of information. I then categorized all the information into different aspects of musical applications (i.e. concentration, stage fright, etc.) and translated the information into an organized resource for musicians to refer.

Now don't get me wrong - I don't feel it's necessary to become a genius to be a good musician. However, if you were to focus on certain mental abilities as they pertain to your needs as a musician, you would improve your musical skills. While writing this book I made it a point not to go too far in depth with the scientific and psychological explanations behind the techniques. Rather, I focused on how to take proven facts about how the mind worked and applied them directly to techniques for improving specific aspects of musicianship. I tried to achieve a blend of detail and simplicity. After all, I doubt any of you are concerned with studying psychology or brain function and therefore I tried to limit the scientific jargon. I assure you that this book is written by a musician for musicians.

Before starting, I'd like to make some suggestions. To get the most out of this book, it might be best to read it twice and use a highlighter to mark important bits of information. You may also want to use a notebook to design your personalized plan for applying the techniques that interest you. As with any process of improvement, focus and be patient. Keep at it and you *will* see results.

2
Motivation

"Nothing great was ever achieved without enthusiasm"...
Ralph Waldo Emerson

I'VE BEGUN THIS book with the subject of motivation because it is probably the most important. The other chapters discuss some very important techniques that can achieve amazing improvement's to one's overall musical abilities, however, if you can stimulate a deep motivation along with the accompanying discipline to work hard, then all the other skills will fall into place. This is not to say that the various techniques taught in this book (improving memory, enhancing creativity, overcoming stage fright, etc.) wouldn't benefit your playing. It's just that these other areas of mind power won't even be put to use if you don't have the motivation to go about learning and applying them to begin with. It is for this reason that motivation and discipline must come first.

I would venture to say that you probably already possess a certain level of motivation since you've taken the time to begin reading this book. This alone demonstrates an overall desire to improve your musical ability. What we're striving for here is creating an even deeper level of motivation than you already possess. Example: a person who practices their instrument an hour a day already has a certain level of motivation, but if you want to obtain an even higher level of musical ability or to become a virtuoso then you will have to strive for a degree of motivation that will require even more hours of practice. This simple statement demonstrates motivation and the resulting skill developed through practice as an almost mathematical correlation.

I've read in many places that the formula for becoming a true musical virtuoso is "10 for 10," meaning ten hours a day for ten years. I'm sure this isn't a hard and fast rule. There are probably many of exceptions to it, but it demonstrates the overall level of dedication that many people have and that you too can develop.

You may be wondering what one can learn about motivation and discipline. You may be thinking if you have it then you have it; if not then you don't. Well, this isn't true. If you have a basic spark of motivation, then you can promote and increase it to a higher level plain and simple. What you need to begin with is the motivation to become motivated. By this, I mean *really* motivated. If you can master this element of mind power, then you can ignite the spark that will eventually lead to great musical talent. I'm

sure you now can see now why I've started with this subject. Simply put, your learning process must start with the
deep desire to learn.

They call it "the bug" and it's said that once it has bit-
ten you, your whole life will center on music. You will constantly think about music and playing. There are many
people who have the desire to become a great musician,
but the most important element here is to have the desire
to **do the work** to become a great musician. You have to
truly want to do the work, not just begrudgingly accept
the fact that the work is necessary and therefore you have
to get it done, like it or not. You will no longer think of
learning and putting in hours of practice as "work", but
instead, look forward to it. Remember, if you can create
a state of mind that makes you think of practicing and
studying music for a few hours a day as the most fun you
can have, then it's only a matter of time before you will
become a great musician.

Of course, I concede there are always going to be days
when even the most motivated player would rather just
"veg" and watch TV, this is where discipline comes in.
Motivation and discipline are two different mental processes. For our purpose, I am going to define motivation
as the actual desire and enjoyment to do the work and discipline as the ability to do the work regardless of whether
or not you enjoy it.

It is possible to work very intensely at something even
if it isn't enjoyable. There are those who want to develop a
talent and possess the discipline to do the work but dread
the many hours of practice. Those individuals are running

entirely on discipline. Developing musical skill with only discipline is a very difficult thing to do unless you can also cultivate motivation. It's much easier to practice five hours a day if it's fun.

I want to clarify something before we go any further with all this talk about practicing for four or five hours a day. Not everyone is going for that intense a level of a musical dedication which is understandable. Many of you just want to become good at your instrument but not necessarily revolve your life around it. I'm mentioning the extreme example of musicianship as something that you can achieve if you want to. You may have different goals. The degree to which you take your level of involvement is up to you.

In this chapter, we will discuss psychology, self-hypnosis, focus, and specific techniques that will allow you to take an interest that already exists and magnify it on an emotional and personal level. These techniques will be divided into several categories that can be learned and applied. First, we'll learn a little about human nature and the basic aspects of motivation that are part of our instinctive survival skills; then we'll learn some general principles of motivation. This is what the motivational instructors teach corporate executives and what personal trainers teach their clients in the gym. Finally, we'll review a list of techniques that will drastically expand your existing interest into a red hot burning desire to do whatever it takes to reach your musical goal.

Humans are loaded with subconscious survival-based automatic programming that affects our thoughts and behavior. This is the automatic pilot that kicks in when one is in danger. It will also whisper warnings to you when you're in certain situations that may negatively impact your life whether they are life threatening or not. The need for instinctive survival behavior may have become less important now that we no longer have to worry about being eaten by bears, but the instincts are still there. In some ways it can be a disadvantage (for instance the fear of being on stage), however, there can also be certain advantages such as goal orientated drives and desires even if they aren't needed for actual survival. With this in mind, we are going to tap into the survival instinct that gives a person the want and desire to take action to achieve a goal; it may not be a survival goal, but your subconscious doesn't need to know that. We want to program our brain into thinking that achieving musical excellence is of extreme importance and that you need to do the work necessary to achieve it.

The professional motivators (like the ones corporations hire to psyche their executives) may not admit it to their clients, but the core of subconscious programming is self-hypnotism. So rather than discuss all the various methods they use to do this I will just cut to the chase and get right to it. To make any deep level changes to your thinking, it will need to be done on a subconscious level. Did you know that you self-hypnotize yourself in a lot of ways without even knowing it? Whenever you keep repeating such phrases as "This math is too hard, I'll never understand it," you are self-hypnotizing yourself. Remember that little story they taught you back in second grade about the little train that tried to get to the top of the hill? He kept saying to himself " I know I can, I know I can." That was a psychologically based lesson in self-hypnotism that you were taught. The educational establishment hired child psychologists to design that lesson and for good reason.

The subconscious is like a computer. It can't figure out anything by itself; it only carries out what is programmed into it. Whether information is right or wrong, the subconscious doesn't know the difference. If you program in a computer that two plus two equals five, then it will always calculate that two plus two equals five. If you program into your subconscious that " I'm stupid and can't understand this math" then it's a proven fact that your natural intelligence will be interfered with. The neurological connections will not be made to understand the math, or it will seem more difficult than it should.

Have you ever seen a nightclub act where a hypnotist makes someone bark like a dog? They are temporarily made to believe that they are a dog. It's been common knowledge for years that you *can* program your mind, we will use this fact a few times throughout this book, though now is probably the most important use for it. We will want to implant a deep desire to spend many hours of work to develop our skill. As I've already stated improving as a musician starts with motivation. After you have developed this everything else (improving memory, enhancing creativity, etc.) is the icing on the cake.

For those of you who are thinking, "While we're at it why don't we just hypnotize ourselves into thinking that we are already great musicians?" Sorry, it doesn't work like that. You cannot hypnotize yourself to speak French can you? Musical skill requires knowledge that can only be learned and dexterity which is built through practice (by developing an electro - chemical path from the brain to the muscles), there are no shortcuts here.

I've decided to focus on self-hypnotism now for two reasons. First, it's an important tool for building motivation. Second, I wanted to establish it early enough so that you can begin practicing it. It may take some people time to get the hang of it. And as with any skill your self-hypnotism technique will improve with practice.

I understand that some people are skeptical about "alternative science" and there are many subjects that raise doubt especially on subjects that stretch one's personal knowledge of the world and reality. However, this isn't like the UFO debate or whether there's life after death. There're hard scientific facts supporting the existence of a subconscious, and it's been proven that the subconscious can be programmed either by someone else or by yourself. This fact has been used to improve athletic performance, overcome the urge to smoke, brainwash people, (as North Korea did to American captives during the Korean War), remove emotional trauma due to tragedy, and entertain (as with lounge acts). The facts are all documented and backed up by research.

Simply put, self-hypnotism is the act of implanting "suggestions" into your subconscious. Your subconscious, as mentioned earlier, is very similar to a computer. It will do what it's told regardless of logic, who is instructing it, or how it's being told. A small child is being hypnotized when they are repeatedly told by thoughtless parents that they are stupid. The child may actually be very smart but their subconscious doesn't know this. Constant suggestions from an authority figure will, over the course of time, program the subconscious and the child will begin to think he is stupid (and act accordingly).

You may have noticed that I've been pointing out negative examples of self-hypnotism. These are suggestions that people implant that limit their skills. Due to human nature and principles of fear and self-doubt (which are survival based instincts) people seem to program mostly negatives into their subconscious. However, positive self-hypnosis works just as well. One can program a positive suggestion that will work just as strongly as a negative one.

Let's first go over some possible concerns regarding self-hypnotism. You should know that it is totally safe, and there's nothing to worry about regarding tinkering with your mind. As I've pointed out (and research has proven), you naturally self-hypnotize yourself every day. What can possibly be wrong with implanting some positive improvements?

Second, don't try to implant too many suggestions at first. Take your time and work with just a few. As you add things to your list, try to focus on only one or two changes you want to make. As you improve with your self-hypnosis you can always brush up on the changes you have already implanted. For now, we'll start with implanting motivation. As you move along with this book, you will eventually change the subject of your daily self-hypnotism from motivation to other things like confidence on stage for example, but you can always return to motivation.

There are many different techniques that have been invented and used to achieve self-hypnosis. The two that

I'll describe are basic techniques, but there are many others. Feel free to read about other methods that you may prefer. Or if you have the cash there are always professional hypnotists that can help you. The drawback of hiring a professional hypnotist is that hypnosis is a gradual thing. The many sessions required to implant a deep personal change will cost a bit of money.

You may be thinking, "if a lounge act hypnotist can make someone bark like a dog wouldn't they be able to implant a change right away"? The lounge act may seem like a firmly implanted suggestion, but it is a very shallow and temporary type of hypnosis that only lasts for a few minutes. The types of deep changes we're going for are permanent and powerful. There are no shortcuts here either. It is a process that will require daily sessions (although they're only 10 minutes long) and may require weeks to take full effect.

Self-hypnosis method #1: This is the most widely used technique. Begin by sitting in a comfortable chair and sit up straight. You are now going to change your brain wave patterns from Beta to Thera. You may ask, "What are Beta and Thera wave patterns?" Here is a quick lesson on brain waves. The brain works on an electrical pulse or wave patterns. Research over the years has determined four major categories of brain waves. Beta is normal consciousness, Alpha is a relaxed state, Thera is a very deep relaxation (the semi-consciousness you feel right before you fall asleep) and Delta is sleep. To communicate with your subconscious, your brain waves must be in the Thera state.

First, totally let go of all tension and let your muscles go limp almost to the point where you can't sit up straight (but continue to sit straight because it's the best position), then use what's called "the escalator method." This is one of the most popular techniques. Imagine being on an escalator going downward. As it gradually takes you lower slowly count backward from ten to one, visualizing each number to be the escalator getting lower and your body and mind becoming more relaxed. All of this is very important and is the fundamental aspect behind hypnosis; you want to achieve a slower brain wave pattern. Once the imaginary escalator reaches one and you feel that you've become very relaxed prepare yourself for an even deeper level. Imagine yourself as being totally weightless. Become aware of a totally relaxed state that has opened up your mind. You now can begin actual one on one communication with your subconscious. Don't under-estimate the importance of the relaxation process. Self-hypnosis doesn't work unless your brain waves are slowed down and your heart rate is relaxed.

Next, you can begin to talk to your subconscious. It isn't at all like talking to yourself. You should think of it as talking to a separate being or mind. Your subconscious may be part of you, but it can be just as cold, calculating, and impartial as a computer. Although your subconscious is a hidden element of your being, you will now have the power to control it and make it work for you. In a state of self-hypnotism, you will be able to tell your subconscious that you are not afraid to play on stage, that you are confident in your ability to reach your goal of musical virtuosity, or anything that you want to have programmed into your "automatic pilot." But for now let's just deal with motivation.

There are two common methods used to talk to your subconscious while under self-hypnosis. You may mentally vocalize statements that describe what you wish to achieve (such as "I have a deep desire to practice my instrument many hours a day"), or you can start a tape recorder (already having your finger positioned on the play button) with a pre-written dialogue of suggestions.

For motivation, a good self-hypnosis suggestion to start with is implanting the desire to practice long hours. Actually having fun practicing, learning theory, doing scales, memorizing songs, etc. Tell your subconscious that you don't think of it as work but as enjoyment. Program your subconscious that you would rather practice than watch TV or hang out with your buddies. Trust me; you won't become a zombie. You can still watch TV and socialize but unlike the past practicing music will be much higher on the list of things that you very much want to do. With this state of mind, how could you not become a great musician? It will only be a matter of time until you achieve your desired result.

Each of your self-hypnosis sessions should only last about 10 minutes. That is all that is needed. When you have completed your session, come out of your relaxed state slowly by stretching, getting up, and moving about. This process may have to be repeated every day (maybe twice a day) for a few weeks before you will see positive effects. For some people, it's quicker. Improvement through self-hypnosis takes time. It won't happen overnight, but you won't notice the time it takes if you make it a daily habit. It will become an ongoing part of your daily routine akin to brushing your teeth. After a few weeks of self-hypnotism (on the subject of motivation) you can move onto another aspect like overcoming stage fright or enhancing creativity, however, it'll be important to reinforce the motivation suggestions now and then.

Self-hypnosis method #2: To start, sit in a chair in front of a mirror. As in the first method, you need to achieve a relaxed state. Once again you can use the escalator method. Once completely relaxed (and therefore in the thera state) stare very deeply into your eyes. You might find this hard to do, and it may create a feeling of uneasiness. You will feel that a wall you usually stand behind is missing. Keep staring until you get the feeling that you are looking into yourself and not just a reflection of your face. You will know what I'm talking about when it happens. It usually takes about 30 to 60 seconds of staring before you feel this. Then you simply speak to your subconscious as if it's another person. Tell it firmly and slowly that you will begin to feel a great motivation to practice, study and do any work needed to achieve your musical goal. Express the subject of your session (in this case motivation) with a number of suggestions - always staring into your eyes. Continue this for about 10 minutes. Then relax your stare, stretch your arms and come back to normal consciousness.

It is important to accept that hypnosis is indeed a fact and that it can be used to implant positive habits and strengths into your subconscious. It will enable you to become dramatically inspired and motivated to practice and study music far more than you otherwise would have.

By itself, hypnosis should achieve an intense level of motivation. I also believe in covering all the bases and taking multiple steps to achieve a certain goal. You will increase your chances of success by doing so. You will notice throughout this book that I list numerous techniques for achieving a certain result even though one may be enough. There's no harm in having multiple tools to use. This way you can choose the one you prefer best or use them all. So let's continue with more methods you can use.

The following is a list of conscious, as opposed to sub-conscious motivation boosters. When used in combination with hypnosis these techniques will help you develop and *keep* a deep permanent incentive to practice and improve your skills. You must always continue to reinforce your motivation, and not just feel that once it's developed it will always carry you through. Don't become overconfident that your motivation will never need reinforcement. Many people have started projects being intensely inspired at first only to gradually lose interest and eventually give up.

Make a list of personal motivators. For example, if listening to Jimi Hendrix or Stevie Ray Vaughn play guitar inspires you then put up their posters next to where you practice. Use whatever motivates you to push you to get through the rough times when you don't feel up to it or are struggling with a particular piece.

Knowing that successful musicians often achieve fame, fortune, and the affection of the opposite sex put up posters of fancy cars and attractive movie stars or models. Keep in mind that this is just an additional form of motivation (and some may think rather shallow), but if it works even a little, by all means add it to your list. Put on your favorite music, sit and listen to it with your head back and eyes closed. Enjoy the feeling you get and remember what it is that drives you to want to be able to play and produce the sounds that bring you such great feelings and energy. Getting distracted by the quest for fortune and fame may cloud the real aim here, but at the very least motivate yourself to become a great musician for the sake of music. In addition to that, you can always add the incentive of acquiring fame and fortune. Your motivation doesn't have to be totally logical so long as it's a strong emotional trigger and it doesn't confuse your ultimate goal.

Read inspirational biographies of successful individuals who struggled initially but persevered to achieve their goal. Sometimes it's good to get advice from a local virtuoso and hear them describe how they kept practicing hour after hour despite various hardships. When you hear about people who kept working hard toward a goal while battling obstacles and dilemmas, it can't help but motivate you to work hard at your goal.

Remind yourself of a recent success like a great performance at a local nightclub's open mic night. Perhaps previous to that gig you practiced especially hard for a few weeks and the result was the best playing you've ever done. Reminding yourself of that accomplishment may motivate you to continue working with even more conviction toward your goal of musical excellence.

Reward yourself after long practice sessions or good performances. Maybe you recorded your favorite TV show while you were practicing. You used self-discipline to postpone watching the show so you could practice, but now that you're done, kick back, relax and watch the show. This is a classic example of "delay of gratification". You did what was important first then rewarded yourself afterward.

I believe that now you should have a solid core of motivational tools to use. As I mentioned before, you need to constantly reinforce your motivation or you may not follow through. You may always desire and daydream about being a great musician, but you have to accept and want to do the actual work required to become great. You must do more than just initiate the motivation. You have to learn how to nourish it, reinforce it, and overcome frustration, burnout, and occasional distraction. Anyone can get psyched on New Year's Eve and resolve that "Starting tomorrow I will begin a diet to lose 50 pounds." Right then and there you may feel genuine motivation but what happens two days later when that special spark of inspiration is no longer felt? As I have pointed out, it's possible to rely on discipline, though many people find this difficult to do. The most effective way to reach your goal is to re-spark that motivation and keep reinforcing it so that it never fades again.

Do not become overconfident that an intense feeling of motivation will always remain. Have you ever fallen out of love with someone whom two years ago you could never imagine not being crazy about? Sometimes feelings fade. The key to keeping the fire of musical motivation burning is constant reinforcement. There is always going to be an occasional day when you just don't want to practice but if you have that feeling two days in a row immediately work on re-sparking that intense motivation that you had previously. Remind yourself of your goal. Review your list of personal motivators. Step up your hypnosis sessions. Do something that will get you psyched again. Go see a particular band play that you know has an amazingly talented musician you admire. Go see that musician play and marvel at his or her skill. Get angry that you can't play like that. Get jealous of their ability. Get frustrated that you aren't at that level of talent when you know you could be with hard work. Take that opportunity to get your motivation fired up.

Motivation is a constant activity. It requires a steady process of maintenance. It can't be thought of as automatic or self-perpetuating. You may have heard about certain musicians who were psyched from an early age, always had the "bug" which never faded away, and then went on to greatness. It is true that some people are so deeply inspired that they need no additional work to rekindle motivation and their desire never fades away. Or perhaps their interest did fade now and then and without noticing it, their determination was rekindled by something or someone. These people are rare. They may have been lucky to be at the right place at the right time, and something or someone helped to keep them focused and motivated. They may have been raised by a musical and nurturing family. My point is that you shouldn't count on your motivation always lasting or being re-motivated automatically.

Motivate yourself and maintain that high level of interest. The road to musical excellence can be supplemented by the other subjects in this book, but motivation must come first.

3
Memory

MUSIC AND MEMORY go hand in hand. The average band has a playlist of about four hours or approximately fifty to sixty songs. That's a lot of memorizing considering all the combinations of arrangements, timing's, melody's, etc. Vocalists have lyrics; instrument players have chord progressions, and then, of course, there's the ultimate memory challenge - the instrumental solo. No other art form is as demanding with regard to memory (perhaps stage actors come close).

The learning process of music theory itself also requires a great deal of memory taking into account the study of scales, chords, notation, inversions, intervals, harmonic progressions, etc. A college course in music can be just as grueling as law or accounting.

Let's first discuss how the mind stores information and how that information is retrieved at will. If you could bear with me for the next few paragraphs, you will see how a lot of this technical stuff will actually apply to improving memory.

To begin, the brain contains about ten billion neurons which are cellular units. Spreading from each neuron are thousands of fibers connecting the neurons to one another. The junction of two of these fibers is called a synapse. There are estimated to be over ten trillion synapses in the brain. It is through the synapse that one neuron interacts with another. Electrical pulses and chemical reactions take place in this tiny space, and this activity is the core of consciousness. There are also certain proteins and other molecules present that if triggered will alter the electrochemical activity. This changing of activity is how memory works.

When you take in information through the senses, it creates a change in the electrochemical activity within the synapse. The more you take in through your senses, the greater the change in the electrochemical activity thus the more solid the memory. To improve memory you have to reinforce and strengthen the molecular changes in your brain's network of neurons. It probably wouldn't do much good if I were to end this chapter here. Now what we must do is to take this and other discoveries about the brain and apply it to the strengthening of memory. Believe me, all of this biology talk is the basis of the techniques that have been designed for memory improvement as you will see later.

There are two types of memory, short term and long term. Short term memory is the temporary storage of information, a tool to help you in your day-to-day living. It's short term memory that remembers the beginning of a book long enough for you to make sense of the end of the book. Later you will eventually transform that short term memory of the book into long term memory but only after certain chemical changes take place in the brain.

Long term memory is permanently implanted into your brain.

A popular misconception is that memory is like a bucket of water with a limited capacity and once it's full some has to be poured out to make room for new water. This is not true. Science has yet to find any limit to how much can be stored in memory. Some studies indicate that you can remember every single second of your conscious life. For example, what you were doing on October 3rd, 2003 at 2 pm. Your mind is like a video camera that's always running.

It's been proven that there are certain people with photographic memories who can read and remember word for word an entire book. These are rare cases and studies have been done to determine if these people have special brain chemistries or if they have simply developed intense mental habits based on effective memory techniques. Testing has proven that these special cases are due to both unique brain function and memory habits. Although you may never be able to achieve their level of memory, you can still dramatically improve your memory using these methods.

Memory can be divided into three actions: Registration - the intake of information, retention - the storage of information, and recall - the retrieval of stored information. To improve memory, all three of these aspects must be worked on.

Act one: Registration. If you are unfocused and distracted when you are memorizing information, it will not be stored properly. In computer terminology this would be called GIGO, for "garbage in – garbage out." If you program into even the most powerful computer that 2 + 2 =

5, then all the information coming out of that computer concerning 2+2 will be wrong. Your brain is a lot like a computer so in many ways you should treat it like one.

The brain is one of nature's most amazing machines, but it is not without its limitations. You can't just quickly and incompletely look at a complex collection of information without taking the time to fully focus and analyze it and then expect to fully recall it later. You must look at something and truly see it if you want to be able to memorize it. This simple fact is one of the most important keys to improving memory, and we'll expand on it here and later in the chapter on concentration.

An effective way to implant information is to analyze it. If you're memorizing a solo, for example, take notice of the scale or scales, the timing, and overall flow. Break it down into sections based on phrasing or riffs. Make a map of its progression based on its location on the instrument (i.e. on guitar a solo may start in A minor at the 5th fret, move up to the 12th, then switch to D major at the 7th, etc.). The more you fully see and think about what you're trying to memorize - the deeper it will be implanted. This is much more effective than just coldly and impartially dealing with what you're memorizing as just bits of information.

Sometimes it helps actually to say the information out loud, read it twice, or do whatever it takes to make the information stand out. If there's a little part of it that you don't understand take the time to find out exactly what is meant. Grab a dictionary if it's a word you don't know. You may think it's just one word and that it isn't important to the overall concept, but you'd be amazed at how sometimes one word will change the whole meaning of a sentence which then can have an effect on the meaning of the overall subject.

The two words to summarize registration are focus and understanding. We sometimes have the habit of thinking that if we understand something 80% - 90%, that it is good enough. Well sometimes it is, but when it comes to memory, especially super memory, you have to 99% to 100% *see* and *understand* it to recall it perfectly later.

When learning information, you have to summarize it. Usually, the books that you are reading on a subject will just present the information. But to fully understand it, thus improving your chances of fully memorizing it, you have to take it a step further. This one principle is para-mount –fully understanding something first. Most people have the habit of thinking, "Good enough; I'm pretty sure I get it." They then proceed with memorizing it, sure that they can fill in any blanks later. This is a big mistake. Let's take the major scale and its modes for example. When I say analyze it I mean re-read it, use it in examples, play the scale and isolate the modes frontward and backward. Learn the intervals in a straight line. Be able to recite the intervals verbally (i.e. Mixolydian mode: full, full, half, full, full, half, full.), know the order of the modes, etc. The mind must first be clear on something before it can make the electrochemical adjustments and synapse network-ing required to store the information. It doesn't physically start the process, or at least completely, until it has some-thing solid to work with. The more definite your under-standing of the information, the more "hooks" your brain has to grab and hold onto.

Act two: Retention. Retention can be a conscious decision, "Let me sit down and memorize this song", or just the mind's subconscious trait of storing everything (or almost everything) it sees. Have you ever noticed that a month later you may recall a trivial conversation you had with a stranger while waiting in line at the store but other times you can't remember your friend telling you to pick them up after work? There are a number of ways to improve retention. The primary way is just to become aware of the fact that you are trying to implant something in memory.

Most people just assume that memory is automatic, and they don't make a conscious effort to memorize something. If you treat memory like an activity, like doing math in your head, then the information is "tagged" and is given a deeper level of retention. This just means stopping what you're doing, focusing, repeating the information, visualizing it, and using other techniques discussed in this chapter. Never assume or be overconfident that you will remember something.

Another basic principle of retention is that you tend to remember that which you are interested in. You would need to try half as hard to remember something dealing with music then information about sewing or flower arrangement (assuming that bores you). This is getting back to focus again. You naturally are more aware of a subject of interest which also leads us back to motivation. You may be interested in music but not necessarily interested in all the work required to become a great musician. If you worked on your motivation and discipline (discussed earlier), it would increase your overall awareness of information that otherwise can become tedious and boring after hours of study. Even for the most enthusiastic music lover, studying advanced theory can be dreadfully mind numbing. If you can psyche yourself to get into it, it will improve your ability to memorize what you are studying.

Overall retention is very dependent on focus. As I mentioned before, if you don't store the information sharply you will be at a disadvantage when you go to retrieve it. Due to this fact, your ability to focus your mind is one of the most important elements needed for a strong memory. Therefore, we should take a good look at our focus skills.

It is not uncommon to be lacking in the ability to sharply focus your mind. One of the most significant mental conditions to be brought to public attention over the past few decades is A.D.D., Attention Deficit Disorder, which is the inability to focus one's attention long enough to learn or memorize information. It is usually related to children probably because a child's classroom learning skills are more important to our society than an adult's mental habits. An adult already having been educated is not as hindered by the condition. As adults, to learn new things and advance our abilities and skills, focus is of utmost importance.

Without going too far into detail on the subject of focus disorders, I want to mention a few ways to compensate for these conditions. To make any real advances in memory, your ability to concentrate is very important. Therefore, if you feel that you honestly need some work at improving your focus I would recommend considering the following options:

Meditation - throughout this book I mention the amazing mental benefits that the ancient art of meditation can have for musicians. In this case, a regular schedule of daily meditation can do wonders for your sharpness of mind and focus skills. Even without using the various memory techniques mentioned here meditation alone can drastically improve your memory. We will talk more about meditation in later chapters.

Concentration Chapter - if memory improvement is one of your more urgent needs, then work with both this chapter *and* the chapter on concentration.

A.D.D - seek specific help for A.D.D. (Attention Deficit Disorder) if you think you have it. There are medications that can be prescribed and other treatments that are now available from professionals. If you truly feel that you have a significant case of attention failure, then this may be one of the most important step's you can take to improve your musicianship.

Nutrition - later I'll deal with diet and nutritional strategies for sharpening the mind. Also mentioned are possible dietary supplements and even pharmaceutical "smart pills" that along with a doctor's supervision can drastically remove those mental cobwebs and improve focus and memory.

Here we have gone over some fundamental memory improvements that can be utilized by everyone in the day-to-day use of memory. Later I'll take these and other techniques and specifically tailor them to musical situations. We'll discuss tips for memorizing songs, solos, and music theory, and deal with ways to incorporate these new habits into your regular musical way of doing things.

Act three: Recall. Recall is the act of retrieving information. This is the important part. After all, what good is implanting information if you can't bring it to the surface again when it's needed.

When you're on stage and playing a melody that you've memorized, the notes that your mind are recalling from memory are put directly into action. You don't think about or analyze the recalled melody; there's no time for that. What you are doing in a case of "playing from memory" is bypassing conscious awareness of the information you are recalling and directly sending the signal to your fingers or mouth. This is called "finger memory" obviously enough.

Other situations are less direct, such as recalling the first half of a solo that you are finishing learning. A case like this will allow you to contemplate the information as you are bringing it to the surface. You can analyze how accurate your memory of it is and see how quickly you are recalling it. You can look at any problem areas your memory has and overall mentally observe your memory in action. It is a good memory improvement strategy to analyze your memory in the recall phase. Take note of what is coming back to you and think about how you had put it into memory to begin with. Look at the big picture of your memory and form conclusions about the things that are being recalled easily and the ways you both implanted and retrieved the information. Memory can be thought of as a skill, and one way to improve a skill is to analyze it, seeing what needs improvement and what techniques are working well. For one thing, I'm personally confident that this is when you will see the techniques listed in this book paying off.

Your ability to recall is better when you are relaxed. In my chapter on confidence, I list various ways to relax, overcome performance anxiety and strengthen your musical self-confidence. Without going too far into detail on the physical reasons why tension interferes with memory let me just point out that stress raises your blood pressure, produces high levels of adrenaline, alters your brain waves (stimulating beta waves and reducing alpha and thera waves), increases levels of ACTH hormones and creates many other brain and nervous system changes.

Stress is designed as a survival tool to give us the increased strength to "fight or run", which is an instinct left over from our early days of evolution when we had to survive against wild animals. Now we rely more on intelligence for survival but our bodies still suffer from these intense physical effects when we are put on the spot, even if that spot is a stage, and we're not in a life threatening danger. This stone-age instinct hasn't evolved with our life in a society. The main drawback of this physical reaction to fear is that memory recall isn't high on the list of immediate fighting skills and due to all that goes on physically it is pushed to the back of your mind. In other words, we become idiots when we're frightened. Just put a gun to somebody's head and ask him his telephone number. (a theoretical proposition, obviously). The conclusion of all this is that your reaction to fear and your stage fright coping skills weigh heavily on your memory ability. For this reason, you should coordinate this chapter with the chapter on confidence later in this book. It is another example of how a lot of these aspects of mind control are inter-related.

Regarding recall, focus is again a critical component of the memory process. Despite how well you put the information into storage if your attention is all over the place when trying to recall information your memory will suffer. This is yet another reason to coordinate the Concentration chapter with this one

Now that we have gone over what is known about memory, and how the brain works to store and recall information, let's start learning some specific tricks that will go a long way in creating a great memory. These techniques can be applied to many situations needed by most musicians.

It has been proven that you store information better later in the day then in the morning. This is due to the body's cycle of hormone and chemical production which results in the mind's memory functions. It is another reason why they say breakfast is the most important meal of the day. You need the nutrients to jump start your brain. If you must study in the morning, start with a good breakfast about an hour before beginning.

When studying or memorizing something use sixty-minute cycles of study then short breaks in between. Five or ten minutes should be fine. Fatigue and tension are major retention blockers. But more importantly, the process of the brain's electrochemical system seems to work in sixty-minute cycles. Once you begin stimulating intense mental activity this cycle peaks and begins to decrease significantly after about 50 to 60 minutes. At that point take a 5 to 10 minute break, get some fresh air, stretch your legs, and maybe eat a quick energy snack - then resume studying. Continue this pattern continuously.

This trick is very important. About an hour after finishing a study session give yourself a quick review and test of the material. Also, review it again 24 hours later. This takes full advantage of the way the brain goes through a consolidation process to permanently implant the protein / chemical/electrical changes that we discussed earlier. This plan is vital: study, wait one hour, review information, wait 24 hours, review the information again. Again – this process is very important and is based on the electrochemical activity of the brain.

A very important technique for developing a super memory is association. Association is the practice of using words or images that you relate to the information that you are having a hard time remembering. The word or image will trigger your recall of the specific information that you have visualized or tagged the word to. For example, you may need to remember a shopping list of the following items: milk, corn, bottled water and aspirin. Rather than remember four separate items you would invent a sentence (the crazier, the better) tying all four items together then visualize it. For instance: A cow eating corn gets thirsty for water and later gets a headache. This absurd concept is easy to remember and is the basis of memory improvement - association. You can come up with many ways to use in for remembering songs or music theory.

The more senses you use in your imagined association, the more "hooks" your memory has to grab onto when you try to recall the information. Use sight, sound, feel, smell and even emotion. What you are trying to do is build one big picture out of separate bits of information. This is the basic process used by all of the renowned memory experts that you see on TV talk shows. We have all seen the guys who will dazzle us by memorizing everyone's name in the audience or who will memorize ten people's Social Security numbers s within sixty seconds. They have definitely taken these memory techniques to a higher level (and in many cases they probably have unique brain chemistries), but the basic method that they all use, regardless of having gifted brains, is association.

A classic example of applying association to actual use is a routine practiced by a great Roman orator named Cicero. What he did to memorize a very long speech was to walk around his house and stop at certain places, maybe the front door, the stairway, wherever. He would then memorize a section of the speech while standing at that location and make a point of associating that section to that location. He would then move to another location and continue with another section of the speech. A path would then be created throughout his house that would remind him of the entire speech. When he then gave the speech in front of an audience, he traveled that path in his mind and remembered one section at a time. He thus associated the familiar surroundings of his house to a long and complex speech.

One of the reasons that children have exceptional memories is that they naturally use imagery to visualize things they remember. We tend to lose this ability as we grow older, and our memory suffers because of it. To sum-marize this very crucial act of memory retention - create an image or images using sight, sound, feel, and emotion to construct an easily remembered image that you can directly translate into the information you are trying to remember.

When studying, we tend to remember the first and last items the most. You can compensate for this by reviewing things in different orders. If you initially study something then review it an hour later and review it again the next day. That would give you three opportunities to arrange the information so that more items stand out in your mind.

Before learning something go through it and deter-mine what you think will give you the most trouble memorizing. It has been proven that we can predict very accurately what we will be able to memorize easily and what will give us trouble. You can then compensate for the difficult parts by making them the first or last item on your list and spending more time on them.

An important aspect of memory is organization. Your memory is a lot like a library. If a library had thousands of books stored completely at random, it would be almost impossible to retrieve any one book, but when books are stored systematically (by subject, title or author), then retrieval is simple and quick. Memory is very similar in con-cept to this system. When information is memorized, you should be conscious of a category or relationship that it falls into. This is another aspect of association. It is just another example of increasing the amount of "hooks" that you will be able to grab onto.

One thing that scientists have proven is that memory is very dependent on emotional and mental states. For example, if you memorize something while in a happy mood you will best be able to recall that information when you are happy. Ever notice on rainy days that dismal memories seem to surface more? If you were to misplace your keys and are frantically looking for them, chances are you are not in the same state of mind you were in when you put your keys down somewhere. If you were to think of the mood or overall feeling you had when you last had your keys, you would be better able to bring back the memory of putting your keys down. You can apply this principle to recalling songs, lyrics arrangements, etc

Here are a few tricks for memorizing music theory. Most guitar players know the old rule for memorizing the open strings: E, B, G, A, E -"Excellent Beginning Guitarists Don't Allow Errors" (you may have used another one). This is a classic example of association. Try this one for memorizing the order of the modes: Ionian, Dorian, Phrygian, Lydian, Mixolydian, Aeolian, Locrian - "I Don't Play Like Malmsteen And Lifeson". This is one I came up with. Yngwie Malmsteen and Eric Lifeson are two of my favorite guitar players, so this worked well for me. But of course, you can invent one that better suits your preferences. The point is - invent a sentence, acronym, or a short story in which to relate the information. By the time you finish a full-scale study of music theory, you may have about 40 of these acronyms. They can be used for all aspects of music ranging from the sharps and flats in each key to the construction of chords (i.e. a minor ninth - 1, b3, 5, b7, 9).

Another method is to invent working examples of what you are learning. If you are learning the major scale, for example, write a melody that's seven measures long, each measure using a different mode of the major scale. Always take what you've learned and construct something with it right away. Memorize your example along with the information. This alone will achieve a higher degree of true understanding, which is one of the most significant memory boosters there is.

Another key element is reviewing and testing. The chemical processes in the brain take about 24 hours to fully develop when you memorize something, although a significant amount of chemical action takes place within an hour after first implanting the information. As I mentioned before, by reviewing the information about 60 minutes later, and again within 24 hours, you'll strengthen the brain's physical storage of what you've learned. With that in mind, either review or take a test (if one is provided in the book you're studying) of the information. If there's no test at the end of the chapter or section, invent your own. For songs, try writing it out backwards or find some other way to test your memory of the chord progression or melody. When you try to recall the information during a test, you're sending all kinds of electrochemical energy through the newly created synapse changes, which strengthen them.

Now let's move on to memorizing songs. The first thing I do before I begin to memorize a song is to tape it on cassette or CD and listen to it as many times as possible. I'll listen to it in the car, while eating, doing the dishes, etc. This will develop a true feeling for the flow of the song

and will most likely implant the memory of the arrangement without even consciously being aware of it. If you
don't have the time to listen to the song repeatedly for a
few days (or even a day), then at least make an effort to
listen to it about five or six times before you begin the
memory process.

The following are steps to take that will guarantee a
thorough, rock solid memory of a song. First, keep a notebook. Start with an index page so you can list all the songs
in that particular notebook. Write down the arrangement
of each song. I usually write the song part (verse, chorus,
lead, intro, etc.) at the left of the page, write the chord
progressions in the middle, then write the number of patterns (a phrase or cycle of chords) or measures on the
right.

One of the biggest memory problems musicians have
is when, for example, verse one and two have four patterns, then verse three is different and only has three patterns. Or the first and last chorus have eight measures,
but the middle chorus has six, etc. So in your outline of the
song, use a highlighter or some other way of bringing your
attention to the different part. Then when you memorize
the song think of that part as being different, and it'll help
you to remember the change of patterns or measures.

And speaking of highlighting, I usually use different colored magic markers to underline the different
parts. For example yellow - verses, blue - choruses, green
- bridges, etc. I usually use red to bring my attention to
problem spots or tricky changes. For one thing, this color

system will help to organize the song into components. Second, it brings up the principle of association once again. If you get used to a certain color symbolizing a certain part, after using this system for a while, you'll begin to associate blue for choruses, yellow for verses, etc. Then in your mind's eye, you can visualize the "color flow" of the song. Like I have mentioned before, the more senses you bring into play, the more "hooks" your mind will have to grab onto. You'll be onstage one night, and as the song proceeds through the different parts, you can almost see the different colored sections as your memory grabs the information. Believe me on this one; this system will help you remember the songs arrangement once you get used to it.

Another great way to memorize songs is to use the trick I mentioned earlier regarding how Roman speakers would walk around their homes and associate different parts of their speech to different locations of their house. This system is a great one for memorizing songs and solos. To avoid confusion, every song you memorize with this method should be done in a slightly different path through your house, yard or friend's apartment, etc. By doing this, you aren't mixing up songs if you relate too many to the same locations. There might be one drawback with this system, and that's carrying your instrument around the house. You don't have to physically play at that location in your house, but maybe before each section just take a walk to that location, or at least think of it as you memorize the section of music on your instrument.

This one may seem simplistic, but it works. It's the technique mentioned earlier regarding memorizing theory. Take a chord progression and make a sentence out of the chord names. For example, Am, D, G, B7, E – "A Dog Goes Berserk Easily". This isn't rocket science and there's some drawbacks, but it can come in handy now and again. You just have to remember the minors, sevenths, etc. Also, I wouldn't necessarily recommend translating these onstage while playing. In a live situation, you could get into trouble translating "Berserk" into B7 on the fly. This system is more for simply helping you to memorize the progression when you have time to sit down and think about it, like during band practice or at home.

This next technique works best for guitar players, although any instrument can take some advantage from it. You most likely already do this to some degree. It's simply to become aware of any geometric patterns that are created when you move through the chord progression or lead. For example B, E7, D, Am (all in root position). The movement through this progression forms a square on the guitar fretboard. Other progressions may form triangles, N's, Z's, etc. If you look at the locations of the root notes and connect the dots, you can form a lot of different shapes that can help you remember the chords. This method is especially handy because it allows you to easily transpose the key you're in by simply moving the whole shape up or down the fretboard. As with the last technique, you just have to make note of the minors, sevenths, and other extensions.

On the piano, things are a little more one-dimensional, but you can still find ways to imagine shapes. The black keys are a big help in visualizing shapes. D-major, for example, is a triangle; a D major 7 is a lopsided rectangle, etc.

Solos become a little more involved. I usually divide leads up into sections, both in terms of musical arrangement and location on the guitar fretboard (or keyboard, etc.). An example of a guitar solo may consist of an intro, a section of building intensity, a melodic and mellow part, a major climax of rhythm and speed, a section of decreasing intensity, and an ending.

For stringed instruments, think in terms of geometric shapes and locations, i.e., the intro starts in the lower fret's, the buildup climbs around the seventh fret, the climax consists of riffs at the 12th fret, etc. I've actually drawn maps of leads, listing the order the sections are in and what kind of action happens at each location. Then it's just a matter of remembering the scale or scales used and the phrasing and riffs used at each section. Drummers and horn players can also visualize movements and progressions with a little imagination. Any means used to visualize motion on the instrument will help the memory of a song or solo.

The last step is to use the techniques that were mentioned earlier regarding the study of theory. Simply apply them to memorizing song arrangements, chord progressions, lyrics, etc. Just knowing more about how memory works and how registration, retention, and recall are interconnected will enable you to develop your own personalized techniques for improving your musical memory.

We've all been hearing a lot lately about "smart foods." It's probably no surprise that your mental clarity and sharpness has a lot to do with your nutritional habits and overall health. Eating junk foods and drinking beer for breakfast is simply the quickest way to weaken your mind and memory. Let's start with diet. First, let me point out that I don't have the credentials to recommend any major dietary changes or overall nutritional advice. What I'm going to suggest is simply a few additions to an already overall balanced diet. Before making any major changes in your diet, you should always check with your doctor or nutritionist. This might sound corny and paranoid, but there have been many deaths due to people following diets that severely weakened their body's immune system and overall health.

The following is a list of foods and supplements that have been scientifically proven to strengthen the brain's electrochemical efficiency and dramatically improve intelligence and memory. You can easily incorporate these into your diet: Apples, Lecithin, B complex (especially B-12), eggs, raisins, nuts, fish, yogurt, potatoes, soybeans, broccoli, zinc, vitamins E and C (specifically "Ester-C"), ginseng, Ginkgo Biloba, calcium, amino acids (in addition to ones already listed), melatonin, choline, niacin, glutamic acid, Q-12, taurine, and about 8 glasses of water per day.

It's important to take these foods and supplements only in a balanced way and as part of an overall healthy diet. For the most part, the vitamins and minerals listed can be found in a good multivitamin and mineral pill. If you really want to take full advantage of mind-empowering foods and supplements, have a nutritionist design a mind power and memory-enhancing diet. The mental sharpness you'll feel, and the benefits to your playing, will be well worth the $100 fee for the doctor.

Things to avoid are excessive alcohol, excessive caffeine, marijuana, sedatives, and smoking. I realize that these things may be hard for some people to quit, but at least reduce their use. It's a proven fact that their use dramatically reduces the brain's ability to absorb oxygen and nutrients. I hate to sound preachy here, but these things are major inhibitors of memory and overall mental sharpness. Sometimes to achieve excellence at a certain activity, sacrifices must be made. Considering the importance of concentration and memory for musicians, you should consider at least a major reduction of certain lifestyle habits.

In addition to nutrition, exercise is a very important activity for any musician to do on a regular basis. Exercise tones the nervous system and improves the flow of nerve impulses from mind to body, thus improving the mind's sharpness and memory. About an hour after a moderate workout, you will notice a sharper mind.

Aside from the research that's been done on specific benefits to the mind from certain foods, there have also been major advances in "physco-pharmaceuticals", which is a huge part of the overall medical and pharmaceutical industry. Many drugs have been developed specifically to enhance mental sharpness, memory, focus, as well as emotional balance and coordination. A brief list would include: RNA, Isoprinosine, Vasopressin, Hydergine, Sulbutiamine, DHEA, and Deprenyl, to name but a few. Most of these are prescription drugs, so if you were interested in trying a "smart drug" then perhaps a visit to the doctor/nutritionist would be an option. That way you can have a complete diet /supplement /pharmaceutical program safely designed for you.

Some people may think that this is taking the quest for musical excellence a bit too far, but why not take advantage of all that science has to offer? This could lead to a new level of "super-musicians". Mozart may have been a natural musical genius and virtuoso, but with the aid of science maybe that degree of talent could be within the reach of us all (although tons of practice will still always be necessary).

For those of you who want more information about smart drugs, here's a newsletter that you can subscribe to Smart Drug News, P.O. Box 4029, Menlo Park, Ca. 94026. And of course, a search of the Internet will also reveal a wealth of information on the subject.

Personally, I've found that just a good diet, vitamin supplements, adjusting my lifestyle, and using the memory techniques described in this chapter have resulted in improved memory and a sharper mind. In conclusion: by applying some, most, or all of the techniques and knowledge that has been presented in this chapter, you will see a dramatic improvement in your musical memory skills. There is no other art form that requires as much memorizing as music, so it's an important element of mind-power to develop if you truly want to become an excellent musician.

4
Confidence

SIMPLY PUT, A musician can have all the talent in the world, but if they believe deep down that they are poor players, they will perform accordingly. Case closed. I'm not sure if modern psychologists understand why humans have the ability to limit themselves by implanting negative suggestions. The whole concept of low self-esteem and its negative effect on human performance seems strange to me. Why should this anti-survival, self-destructive tendency even exist? Despite all my research, I can't find any practical explanation for its existence. But despite whether it makes sense or not, we humans have the ability to create subconscious programs that limit our abilities, talents, and performance. As musicians, we are affected by these strange subconscious implants in a very large way.

Imagine being with a professional hypnotist, with a small audience watching, and you are playing your instrument perfectly. The hypnotist then puts you through a session of hypnosis, instructing your subconscious that you are an absolute beginner at playing a musical instrument. You then get back on stage, start playing, and sure enough, you sound like the first day you ever touched the instrument. You can't remember things that you should know like the back of your hand. Your fingers won't do what you tell them to; you can barely play. As far-fetched as this may sound, it is similar to what happens when a musician has low self-esteem of themselves and their musical abilities.

The lack of normal confidence and a poor self-image is just as powerful within the mind as the abilities it blocks. You may as well have not even practiced all those years if you have a subconscious program instructing your mind that you can't play well.

Another mental obstacle is fright. It'll usually happen when you get on stage or in any type of public performance situation. Fright is a survival mechanism that is designed to release adrenaline into our blood systems for added strength to help us fight off attackers or run from tigers. Somehow, through the course of evolution, it became inter-connected with non-life-threatening situations like being in the spotlight in front of a group of people. When you're on stage playing music, you really don't expect the audience to pull out guns and start firing. There's no survival threatening reason for fear. Yet we still feel just as frightened as if being chased by an axe-wielding maniac. (To anyone who has experienced intense stage fright, you know this is not an exaggeration).

These two mental obstacles, self-doubt and fear, are probably the most crippling weaknesses that the average musician has to work on. All of the other components - memory, concentration, etc., are also important, but overcoming self-doubt and fear are absolute necessities for many musicians. Some musicians are so limited by these mental obstacles that they actually stop performing. If you are seriously affected by these conditions, then it is an absolute necessity that you learn the skills for controlling them.

To overcome stage fright and low musical self-confidence, we will work with the following: self-hypnosis, creative visualization, mental anchoring, subconscious triggers, positive thinking, biofeedback, and the science of mental/physical relaxation.

Before dealing with specific attacks of stage fright, I will focus on the more general aspects of everyday musical low self-esteem. To a certain degree, it's the underlying lack of musical confidence that leads to stage fright and the reduction of your ability to perform at your full potential. If you think about it, when you get on stage (or play in front of people anywhere), there is that little voice that says, " I hope I don't forget the chord changes," or " I hope I can follow the rhythm," etc. That little voice is what leads to fear. And once the fear sets in, your mind's focus is cut in half, and there is a good chance you will indeed forget the chord changes or mess up the rhythm. But if you are absolutely confident that you know the chords and can play the rhythm, then fear has nothing to really work with. There is only the element of self-consciousness that can make you nervous even if you were just to stand on stage in front of a lot of people. This chapter will deal with specifics of stage fright later. For now, half the battle is establishing a deep level of overall self-confidence.

For many people, self-confidence and self-image are personal elements that need improving, whether they play an instrument or not. In fact, you may not be able to develop a musical self-confidence if you have a general lack of confidence. At this point, you need to be honest with yourself and admit if your self-image is a weak one because it may be impossible to develop a strong musical confidence if you have an underlying lack of personal confidence. For the sake of covering all the possible scenarios, we'll first deal with confidence and self-esteem on a personal level. We'll then apply this knowledge to musical aspects.

One note before we start, even very confident people can lack musical confidence. You may have developed a strong self-image from a young age, but much of that has to do with early childhood social successes, positive affirmations from your parents or friends, and other situations that made you feel strong about how you look, talk, interact, etc. But now you're in a new ballpark, and you may not have your parents to build up your ego or friends giving you positive feedback. Personal charm and looks is one thing but playing a musical instrument or singing is something else. There is no guarantee that a confident person will be confident about their musical ability. For this reason, we'll cover all the bases in dealing with self-confidence.

Developing a strong self-image is the result of positive thinking and gradual self-hypnosis. Keep in mind that self-hypnosis does not only refer to a ten-minute session of implanting suggestions into the subconscious. Every time you tell yourself things like "I'll never be able to play this song, it's too hard" you are self-hypnotizing yourself. Over the course of years, these negative thoughts will create a rock solid program in the mind that will limit your abilities and performance. You simply have to develop a habit of positive thinking to benefit from gradual self-hypnosis.

For many people, negative thinking is a habit. They've been doing it for so long; they aren't even aware that they do it. Usually, there was something that happened when they were young that first planted the seed of self-doubt. Some cases can be very traumatic like children raised by abusive parents. Other times it is something silly like having a bad day playing kickball which caused the other kids to tease them and tell them that they were not good (even if just at kickball). That is all that is needed to create that little voice inside that says "You're not good (at kickball, or whatever)." Depending on the person these childhood experiences can then lead to other self-doubting feelings that may then escalate into over-all poor self-esteem.

You simply have to think about all the talents you have and realize that the things you aren't good at can be improved if you tried. Once you believe that, and I mean really believe that then you can stop the negative thinking habit and replace it with positive thinking.

Start by catching yourself whenever you think negative thoughts like "I'm not good at parallel parking. I'll never be able to park there". Whenever you catch yourself thinking a negative thought, instantly replace it with a positive one, like " It may be hard, but I know I can park there with a little focus and effort." Keep catching and replacing negative thoughts. After a while, it'll become a habit. The thing about habits is that you can deliberately create them if you desire. The mind will just begin to put certain things into automatic mode, and you won't have to manually think of them anymore.

This process of positive thinking is in itself a form of self-hypnosis. It'll be gradual, but it'll still have the same effect as a hypnotist implanting a positive self-image into your subconscious. In addition to positive thinking, begin a schedule of daily self-hypnosis. We've discussed self-hypnosis in the Motivation chapter, and I'll expand on it again later in this chapter.

Also, if you want to develop the skill further, there are plenty of books and websites on the subject of self-hypnosis. Later I'll introduce other forms of hypnosis, such as Hypno-cybernetics and creative visualization. Whatever technique you want to use, just try to do it every day. It might take a few weeks before you begin to see results but keep doing it. You wouldn't give up practicing your drum exercises because you didn't see results two days later and self-hypnosis is no different. Just keep doing it and wait. You'll see. In addition to developing an overall personal confidence, you can then work on your musical confidence.

But first, let's be realistic. If you honestly know that your playing needs work, then you won't begin to play great by just being confident. The goal here is to stop the mind from limiting the abilities that you've already developed. You won't be able to improve past the point you've already established with hard work and practice. There's no shortcut to skill and talent. A high level of confidence only allows you to play at full potential. A lack of confidence can cut your potential in half when you're on stage. You still have to become good at your instrument the

old-fashioned way, with practice. This is the first, and logical, step to musical confidence - knowing deep down that
you are indeed good. And by good I don't mean you have
to be great, just skilled enough at a minimum level to be
acceptable for a given situation.

Ok, now you've made progress. You've worked at making positive thinking a habit, and you've performed daily
self-hypnosis for a few weeks or months. You can definitely see the results and truly feel good about your playing. Whether you think you still need improvement to your
playing or not, you know you can play to your full potential and know you're able to keep building your talent by
continuing to practice. But now comes another major mental obstacle - stage fright. By overall improving your self-
esteem and musical confidence, half the work is already
done. If you were to get onstage in front of 100 people, you
would definitely be better off already having developed
personal and musical confidence, but unfortunately, stage
fright goes a little deeper. Like I said before, even if you
were just to stand on stage in front of 100 people, there
is something in human nature that causes us to feel intimidated and tense. We now have to deal with overcoming
that sense of fear caused by being the center of attention.
We'll divide this task into two procedures: self-hypnosis
(once again) and practice. Let's start with practice.

There's a reason why piano teachers schedule recitals for their students. It's to get a student accustomed to
playing in front of people. Performance is a major part of
music. The purpose of music in the first place is for other
people to listen to it. No one (or very few people) will
learn a musical instrument just to play it all alone. Even

if you have no plans to become a professional performer, there's still always times that you will play in front of people - around the campfire with a guitar, at the piano playing "Silent Night" at Christmas time when the relatives are over, or open mic nights at the local tavern. If you think about it spending a lot of time and effort to learn an instrument and never play for people is almost strange. Music can be self-entertainment, but it's usually a performance art. So playing in front of people is an aspect of music that teachers try to develop early on when they plan recitals for their students.

The thing about performing in front of people is that it does become easier with time. So if you try to plan as many performances as possible, these experiences go a long way toward developing stage confidence. There are many ways to plan performances: open mic nights at the corner night club, jamming with some friends (there's always a few people sitting around watching), or just playing for people when they come over to visit. Simply play for people every chance you get. Maybe start with friends; you will feel more relaxed in front of people who are supportive. Then you can build your way up to the local tavern's open stage. It's usually on slow nights in the middle of the week that clubs have open mics, so there's usually not too many people in the audience.

When you make the transition to playing for strangers, there are a few tips that can strengthen your confidence. Depending on your personality, some of these may help a lot. First, you know you're good enough to at least play some simple songs on stage (otherwise, you wouldn't have gotten to the point of even attempting to play on stage). You know you're good enough, so don't care if they think you're great. Some of the greatest artists of all time were mediocre players. John Lennon readily admitted he was a very mediocre guitar player. Neil Young is considered a God by many people, yet his singing wouldn't be considered all that great. Don't worry about being super-skillful. To the average person, someone strumming a few simple chords on a guitar can be very entertaining. You don't have to be a virtuoso to entertain people. You'd be surprised how easy it is to sound acceptable to the average listener.

Second, if your level of mind control is capable of it, totally block the presence of the audience out of your consciousness. Have you ever been focusing so intensely on reading a book or watching TV that you couldn't hear someone calling your name or trying to get your attention? This deals with concentration, which you'll learn how to develop in the Concentration Chapter. Muster the best level of concentration you're capable of and focus on other things. Totally focus on setting up your gear, find just the night position on stage that's comfortable, situate the order of the songs you're going to play, then play. Focus 100% on the chord progressions, the melody lines, lyrics, etc. When it comes to aiming the mind, you can never remove awareness; you can only replace it. Don't try to stop the awareness of the audience, but rather attempt to replace it with the awareness of other things (and what better thing than the music you should be focusing on to begin with).

Another strategy is just to don't give a damn. Who cares what anyone thinks about your playing? Be cocky and sure of yourself. The people in the audience are people just like you. Who cares what they 'think? This approach may seem a little brash, but it will help remove the intimidation you feel from the audience. Also, don't care about how great you sound to the audience. This doesn't mean you'll play sloppy because you don't care at all about how you sound. But play good because you want to play good, not because you think the opinions of people you don't even know count.

That last tip may not appeal to someone who's trying to develop a friendly stage presence and communication skills with the audience. Some performers are very concerned with creating a complete show where they talk and interact with the audience. They consider just getting up and playing to be a lame performance, and feel it necessary to create "oneness" with the audience. This is a good goal, and for a professional entertainer, an appropriate one. However, if you're just starting out and are trying to overcome stage fright, then projecting a personality and communicating with the audience can wait until later. For now, you just want to do whatever is needed to overcome fear and play the music without being so nervous that your fingers aren't hitting the right notes.

The second part of our plan requires our old friend, self-hypnosis. At this point, I'm sure you've concluded that I believe the ability to program the subconscious mind to be a major tool in developing the mental skills required by musicians. Self-hypnosis can do in months what conscious effort would take years to achieve. If there's one major breakthrough psychology has made in the past century, it's that the subconscious mind rules the conscious mind and that the subconscious mind can be quickly reprogrammed, just like a computer. All you need is to know how.

Although we discuss self-hypnosis a few times in this book, let me summarize things here and add a few more elements and techniques:

Relaxed vocalized suggestions - Using various relaxation techniques, slow your mind and body down so that your pulse is about 60 bpm (very relaxed) and so your mind is operating at a pulse of about 4 to 7 bps (very tranquil). I personally do self-hypnosis when I first wake up or when I'm drifting off to sleep. This way I can reduce the time it takes to achieve a super-relaxed state. The reason for needing to be very relaxed is that the subconscious mind can only be reached when the brain is functioning slower than eight bps. Once you know you are very relaxed, then simply think verbal thoughts that suggest the things you want to achieve. Think verbal sentences that suggest the skill or habit that you want to be implanted. Also, it's important to know that you can't suggest a negative action, only a positive one. For example, if you want to overcome stage fright, don't suggest - "I will stop being scared on stage", but instead "I will start being confident onstage". Research has shown that the subconscious mind doesn't understand the concept of stopping something, only starting something (or replacing one thing with another). Try to repeat suggestions over and over for about ten minutes per session. Try to perform at least two sessions daily and continue for as many weeks or months it takes to be totally satisfied with the results. Then continue with occasional sessions to help maintain the gains you've made.

Creative visualization - Become relaxed, as mentioned previously, but instead of using verbal sentences, use your imagination to create a very lifelike scene, imagining yourself doing the skill you want to achieve (in this case, being totally confident and without fear on stage). This is a type of daydreaming, but with a definite goal. It's very important to make the imagined scene as realistic as possible. If the situation is being on stage at a nightclub, then imagine the smell of cigarette smoke, the sounds of people talking and playing pool in the background, the feel of the heat from the lights, etc. What you are trying to do is fool the subconscious mind into believing that you already have a certain skill. The subconscious mind cannot tell the difference between reality and imagination; that's why you will wake up from a bad dream out of breath. Your subconscious mind thought the dream was really happening, and your pulse and breathing were raised as if it was real. Make the imagined scene as real looking and sounding in your mind as possible or it won't work as well.

Proceed with the visualization and imagine playing perfectly on stage, having a good time, lost in focus, and at times only half aware of the audience. Work very hard at this mental re-creation. Realize that it's not an immature daydream, but a scientifically proven technique for implanting a power into the subconscious.

After doing these types of sessions for a few weeks, the subconscious will believe that you truly have the confidence to play on stage, and it will become a reality. This also demonstrates a basic principle of human behavior - the best way to change is to act as if you have already changed. The mind will eventually catch up with the act, and it will become a fact. Creative visualization simply takes this principle and applies it to the subconscious.

Hypno-cybernetics - This is a very interesting technique that can be used with any type of self-hypnosis. It's also called finger levitation. It's been concluded that the subconscious is at its most accessible state after it has performed a physical action. For example, if you have the habit of nail biting, it's the subconscious, not the conscious mind, that reaches your hand up to your mouth and bites a nail. The whole concept of a habit is that the subconscious mind has taken over the performance of a physical (or sometimes mental) act. You may find yourself biting your fingernails without even being aware of having lifted your hand up to your mouth.

Research has demonstrated that immediately after the subconscious mind has performed a physical action; that is when it is most exposed and can be reached. At this point, you can take advantage of the opened subconscious and communicate with it. There have been many techniques developed to exploit this fact, but the one I find most effective and easy to perform is finger levitation. This technique has been documented in the book "Hypno-cybernetics" by Maxwell Maltz, M.D. (Bantam Books).

To demonstrate how the subconscious can control the body, try the following experiment. Sit upright in a chair, eyes closed, with both arms bent at the elbows aiming forward (as if on armrests). Go through the process for entering a super-relaxed state. Then use the full strength of your imagination to visualize one arm holding a heavy weight (pulling the arm down) and the other arm holding a cord attached to a large helium balloon (pulling the arm up). Try to keep your arms level, but with your imagination feel the full effect of one arm being pulled down and the other being pulled up. After about five minutes open your eyes and look at the level of your arms. You will see one arm a lot higher than the other despite the fact that you were consciously trying not to move them nor did you even feel them moving.

This is a demonstration of how the subconscious mind can actually take control of the body. With this phenomenon in mind, here is the procedure for Hypnos-cybernetics (finger levitation): First, sit in a chair and place your arms on your legs or arm rests. Chose a finger, perhaps the index finger of your writing hand and point it straight out and level, curling the other fingers under your palm. Then follow the usual procedures for creating a super-relaxed physical and mental state. Second, visualize a string attaching a large helium balloon to your pointed finger. Imagine, with all the mental power you can muster, the finger being pulled very, very slowly upward. Try to consciously keep the finger level despite your mind's view of it being pulled upward. You shouldn't move the finger with your conscious mind because true contact with the subconscious only happens when the subconscious overpowers the conscious mind. After about five minutes, slightly open an eye and quickly glance at the finger.

Chances are you'll see that the subconscious mind has lifted the finger upward. It might take some practice to get the finger levitated about an inch, but even a half-inch is okay. If your finger is indeed lifted, then close your eye again. At this point you are in direct contact with the subconscious and any suggestions you wish to implant will have a lot more effect. Proceed with your self-hypnosis, using the guidelines already established.

Another way to implant suggestions into the subconscious is with repetitive positive thinking. We've already discussed the effect of consciously telling ourselves things and how this gradually implants a program into the subconscious mind. This can take years if only done during occasional situations that arise. For example "Darn, it's going to be hard, but with patience and focus, I know I can play this song". But if you were to do this 20 or 30 times a day, you can greatly increase its effect. There's a lot of time during the average day when you are just sitting there with nothing to do and nothing on your mind (in a traffic jam, waiting in line at the bank, etc.). Try to fill in these periods of nothingness with a constant barrage of positive affirmations ("My piano playing is getting better and better. I'll do great at next week's recital"). This may not have the same power as a full self-hypnosis session (where you enter the thera state), but unlike the once or twice daily hypnotic sessions, it has the advantage of frequency. You can think positive affirmations as an everyday habit, and they can add up to hundreds by the end of the week. These affirmations gradually take effect, and in addition to regular self-hypnosis, will greatly contribute to re-programming the subconscious.

As I have pointed out previously, always catch yourself when thinking a negative thought, then replace it with a positive one. For example, "I'm no good with tools, no wait, I *am* good with tools. I just have to focus and take my time, and I'll be able to assemble this bike. I can do it.." But in addition to this habit, create a dialogue of self-talk that constantly thinks positive thoughts.

In addition to the various techniques of self-hypnosis, there's another subconscious tool that can be used; this is called anchoring." Have you heard of the experiment performed by the Russian psychologist, Ivan Pavlov? His research demonstrated how animals (and humans) could be conditioned mentally. He used a group of dogs and over the course of a few weeks he would ring a bell right before they were fed. The dogs became so accustomed to hearing the bell ring right before eating that eventually just the sound of the bell alone would cause them to salivate. This is a perfect example of anchoring.

To put this into use, you have to associate a physical act with a mental state that you want to trigger. For example snapping your fingers and saying the affirmation "Focus, confidence, success," could be a cue that puts you into a super-focused confident state of mind right before going on stage. To implant a trigger simply use self-hypnosis to tell the subconscious that a certain act (like snapping the fingers) used with a certain phrase (like "I am confident and relaxed") will create a certain reaction (like relaxation or confidence). You'll have to repeat these sessions for several or many weeks, but it will work if you keep at it. When using a trigger, make sure to perform it exactly how you implanted it. Don't be vague. The subconscious is very literal and doesn't assume anything. You have to use the exact combination of physical act and verbal phrase every time.

With all techniques of subconscious implanting, this will take some effort and practice. Once firmly implanted into the mind this trigger will be as effective as when professional hypnotists use it. Usually, these hypnotists implant a trigger to cause an audience member to do something, like automatically standing up, when the hypnotist snaps his fingers. This is no act (well, there's always the occasional phony out there) and as amazing as it may seem, you too can take advantage of this phenomena by implanting a trigger to boost your stage confidence and focus right before going on stage.

Thus far in this chapter, we've mainly discussed confidence and focus - which are mental states. Being onstage also creates physical symptoms like shakiness and sweating. For the most part, once you've made significant changes to your mental habits before and during performances, then the physical systems will take care of themselves. However, it's always best to attack a problem from every angle and not just assume that dealing with the main issue will result in total success. To totally deal with stage fright it's also wise to develop certain physical habits.

The main cause of nervousness is improper breathing. Our bodies automatically deal with danger by restricting the oxygen to the lungs and thus to the blood system. This tends to strengthen the muscles temporarily so that we can run or fight. You may have noticed a weightlifter tightening his breath when about to lift a heavy weight. If you think about it, whenever you have to exert any physical force, you don't breath calmly, but you hold your breath (or tighten and restrict it) during the action. Remember that a lot of these traits are still with us from our prehistoric past despite evolution. This is what the subconscious mind does to us when we perceive danger. And as mentioned before the subconscious mind can't tell the difference between real life-threatening dangers and the possibility of social embarrassment, which is the worse that can happen onstage (unless there're rowdy bikers in the audience who will beat you up if you mess up their favorite song). So in addition to overriding this subconscious error with self-hypnosis and positive thinking you can also learn how to control your breathing.

Relaxed breathing will loosen the muscles, lower your blood pressure, sends the proper amount of oxygen to the brain and allows your digestive system to function (which stops when you're tense which in turn has a big influence on how you feel). All of this results in a good feeling. Feeling good physically will also affect your mental state just as your mental state will affect how you feel physically. It's a cycle that is best to control from both sides to guarantee success.

We've discussed relaxed breathing elsewhere in this book (regarding achieving the proper state for meditation and self-hypnosis), but here is a list of relaxed breathing techniques that can be used in everyday situations. One of the most common techniques of effective breathing is to focus on exhaling and to let inhaling come naturally. Once you've exhaled and pushed out the stale air and carbon monoxide, your lungs will naturally seek to equalize with the outside air pressure and fill back up with air. By letting this happen naturally, you will allow your lungs to develop the habit of relaxing and accepting the intake of air which creates a more effective and natural process. This is the basic principle that's mentioned in all yoga and breathing books.

Now that we've narrowed the process down to just exhaling, you should try to develop exhalation that is slow and long. For most situations where you are not engaged in increased physical activity, like walking fast or carrying amplifiers up a stairway, your exhale should last about four to five seconds. If you're used to breathing a lot quicker than that (which is one reason you may be prone to nervousness), this may seem difficult at first, but with practice it will become easy and natural. Slow breathing is the key to relaxation.

Next, always breathe from the lower lungs (stomach area) and not the upper chest. This is one of the leading causes of tension. The lungs are shaped like pears - they are narrow at the top and wide at the bottom. By breathing from the wide part, you are increasing the amount of oxygen that eventually gets into the blood system. Also, it's important to get rid of the stale air and carbon monoxide, and when you exhale from the large part of the lungs, you are pushing out greater amounts of this useless (and harmful) gas.

It's also important to achieve a good rhythm of breathing: exhaling, relaxing while the lungs fill back up, exhaling, etc. As with many new habits you are trying to develop, this just takes some practice.

Some people may feel that paying attention to their breathing isn't wise and that it's something that you shouldn't tamper with. But people have been "consciously" improving their breathing for centuries and making major improvements to their health and lives. After all, the shallow, quick breathing that you may have developed into a habit is by no means natural. So by consciously replacing that bad habit with a new and healthier technique, you are getting back to what nature intended. Watch a baby breathe and you'll see his or her stomach going up and down, fully and slowly (unless they're upset or excited of course).

Proper breathing is said to be one of the most dramatic improvements that you can achieve. Many books have been written on the subject, and the ancient art of yoga is very focused on the major benefits of breathing. There is even a specialized form of yoga, called Hatha Yoga, which deals specifically with this very important science. I've read accounts of people who claim that developing proper breathing has changed their entire lives. They claim to feel more energetic, focused, relaxed, and their immune systems are much stronger than before. As far as how this can apply to musicians, it seems that this one technique alone could do wonders for improving your mind and body in ways that can dramatically benefit your playing; especially on stage.

If you want to research this subject more, try your local library. It is usually listed under conscious breathing, complete breathing, yoga (pranayama), or relaxation. The Internet also has many sites dedicated to proper breathing.

Another very common technique that has grown in popularity over the past few decades is biofeedback. It is performed in a special clinic that is equipped with electrical devices that measure a person's brain waves, pulse, and other physical energies. This allows the person to see how their body is reacting when they tense up, relax, laugh, get angry, etc. With this ability to monitor their body, a person can practice the ability to achieve certain physical states (usually relaxation). By seeing the meter react to your muscle tension and breathing, you can learn how to control your body by practicing what you could not visualize before.

These biofeedback sessions are not inexpensive, however, and it can sometimes take months of practice to develop the mental/physical coordination that will allow you to relax at will. If you have the financial means, and a biofeedback lab is nearby, then by all means try it out. It is a great way to learn how to control nervousness and tension. I personally feel that meditation and self-hypnosis will achieve the same result but some people claim amazing results from biofeedback, and it certainly should be considered an option.

What we are dealing with here are the methods for controlling the physical effects of anxiety. Of course, this is only half of what causes stage fright. However, it is far better to deal with fright when your nerves feel solid and steady than when you're shaking. This section is merely covering the physical effects of stage fright and ways to reduce the body's unstable, uncomfortable reaction to fear.

One of the biggest obstacles that fear creates for a musical performance are shaky hands. An actor doesn't have to worry about this, but a musician has to have total control over their hands in order to play their instrument. Singers are also affected and find that nervousness can cause their voices to shake.

Sometimes just knowing that the nervousness of stage fright will interfere with your dexterity can cause an additional level of fear, known as double anxiety, which is the fear of fear. It's bad enough to feel anxious about getting up on stage in front of people. But add to that the fear of not being able to play your best because your hands are shaky, and the whole experience will escalate to an even higher level of panic.

This leads us to the next area of focus: proper diet and reducing chemicals that lead to unstable nerves. It's fairly obvious that five cups of coffee won't help matters if you have a problem with nervousness. The thing about nervousness is that it tends to drain the body of energy, thus making people crave stimulants to bring their energy level back up, which can lead again to nervousness. You can see how this will create a vicious cycle. We discuss nutrition and lifestyle elsewhere in this book, usually regarding mental clarity, but the nervousness of stage fright and your bodies overall ability to remain relaxed and energetic has a lot to do with the chemicals you ingest. As before, I'm not claiming to be a nutritionist, and I don't have the credentials to design a complete diet that is tailored to reducing nervousness and increasing energy. However, I have done allot of research into this field, specifically for our purposes here, and have come up with a list of nutrients and supplements that can be safely incorporated into an already healthy diet.

Before listing my findings, it's important to mention that it might be well worth the cost of consulting a certified nutritionist to have a diet, along with prescribed supplements, custom-designed to steady nerves, promote a calm energy level, and improve confidence. Don't underestimate the importance of diet. People have found that by making major adjustments to their diet, along with some supplements, that they have become a new person mentally. The chemicals in your blood stream have every-thing to do with your mental abilities. With that in mind, a scientifically designed diet, and possibly a supplement or two, can promote very steady nerves and inner calm-ness. Once you reduce the physical effects of fear: shaki-ness, cold sweats, hyperventilation, dizziness, nausea, and hypersensitivity (when you can feel every hair on your body), then your ability to focus on the mental techniques of building confidence is greatly improved.

Here is a list of products that can cause nervousness and overall anxiety:

Caffeine: too much caffeine, even in the morning, can have results later that night when you are on stage.

Sugar: Refined sugar is a health hazard, plain and sim-ple. About stage fright, too much sugar in your diet can rattle your nerves.

Sodium (salt) - another health hazard and is also bad for the nerves.

Tobacco- I'm an ex-smoker, so I know how a cigarette seems to steady the nerves. But any doctor will tell you that the only reason smokers feel calmer after a cigarette is that the body begins to crave the nicotine, and when the craving is satisfied, you then feel physically relieved, giving you a feeling of calmness. Smoking has many nega-tive effects on the central nervous system. The chemicals in cigarettes interfere with the brain's neurotransmitters and other functions of the brain and nervous system. Translation, think of all the practice you did to achieve musical accuracy and speed then think of about 20% of all that work being wasted due to the reductions placed on the nervous system by smoking. The next time you're having a craving because you haven't smoked in a few hours, hold out your hand and see how steady you can keep it. You will see the effects of nicotine with your own eyes.

Alcohol: It's often been assumed that a few drinks before a gig can steady the nerves. I'm not totally against this, but too much immediately before getting on stage can fog the mind and screw up a performance. Moreover, too much alcohol overall has been proven to weaken the nervous system. Have an alcoholic try to hold his hand out and keep it still and steady. You can imagine what shaky hands can do to musical dexterity. Don't rely on drugs or alcohol to give you confidence. All it is doing is numbing fear, not removing it. It's far better to work at building confidence mentally than just to get into a drunken state where you're too foggy to feel your fears.

Medicines: Aspirin, antacids, and antibiotics, at high levels, are known to lessen the steadiness of the nerves. Stay well within the recommended dosage, and don't take more than one of these in any one day.

Processed Foods: the additives and preservatives in processed foods are known to be detrimental to calm nerves. Chemicals such as benzyl peroxide, diethyl pyro-carbonate, monosodium glutamate, to name a few. A diet designed to overcome stage nervousness would be based around all natural foods, with only the occasional TV dinner or fast food.

Other food products: an addition to the above rule of "natural foods only" would be to limit saturated fats, foods high in cholesterol, and white flour. Also, pesticides used on fruits and vegetables should be thoroughly washed off before eating. The chemicals in these pesticides can unsteady the nerves.

Now that we've discussed the things to stay away from or reduce, lets list the various vitamins and minerals that are known to promote steady nerves. Once again, I'm not a nutritionist, and you shouldn't run out and buy large doses of these vitamins and supplements without being aware that even vitamins can be dangerous if taken in disproportionate amounts.

I'm going to list these items just to make you aware of the supplements that can be a part of your diet: amino acids (vitamins C, A, E, hydergine, BHT, cysteine, 2-NEA, selenium); wheat germ, phosphorus, pantothenic acid, B vitamins-specifically B1 and B5; calcium, manganese, potassium, iron, folacin, inositol, and magnesium.

A few overall dietary habits would also include drinking a lot of water -about eight glasses per day (very good for the nerves), and increasing the levels of starch and fiber in your diet. Also, it's been proven that eating 5 or 6 smaller meals every day instead of three large meals is good for the nervous system.

Although these physical and dietary habits are important tools, the mental techniques found in this chapter are probably still the best way to achieve musical self-esteem and overcome stage fright. The mind affects the body just as much as the body affects the mind. The next time you get goose bumps from watching a movie or seeing something emotional or intense, look at those little bumps on your skin and see first-hand how your mind directly affects your body. Then, take that example and recognize that by controlling your mind, you can also control your body with regard to the effects of stage fright and nervousness. Then in addition to the techniques of mental conditioning, add a good diet along with certain vitamins and supplements. These things will improve the body's nervous stability. Next, use the discipline to remove certain habits such as smoking and excess sweets, which greatly impairs the nervous system. This is a three prong approach will attack the problem of stage fright from all angles.

Some musicians may disagree with all this talk about controlling stage fright. They'll claim that stage fright is necessary for creating the energy to perform with intensity. I disagree with this, although I'm not suggesting that you should be totally relaxed onstage either. The ideal physical and mental state is a combination of excitement, confidence, and concentration. Fear of any type will not give you the productive kind of energy that will boost your musicianship and your stage presence, but rather will interfere with them. Energized excitement, on the other hand, can motivate you to play at your best and gives you the strength to perform at full intensity.

For some people, self-hypnosis might take many weeks (as opposed to just a few) before showing dramatic results. Don't give up. If you were lifting weights and didn't see large muscles in a few weeks, it certainly wouldn't mean that with continued effort you wouldn't eventually see results. The mind is no exception. You can't give up on these methods if you don't see significant results a week later. We as musicians should know how constant practice gradually achieves results.

The next time you see a performer on stage, and they appear comfortable and at ease, remember that they have the same brain chemistry and nervous system as you and I. Their brains have been conditioned to process the external stimuli of being in front of many people combined with the mental and subconscious conditioning of positive thinking, self-esteem, and confidence. Translation: If they can do it so can you. It's all mental conditioning. See you on stage.

5
Learning

ANY SERIOUS MUSICIAN knows that you never truly reach a point where there's nothing more to learn about music. To the contrary, as you become more advanced and serious with music, you'll probably become more and more aware of new levels of knowledge that can (or should) be learned. Therefore, music can be treated as a life-long study. Not every musician may find this chapter important. Many musicians feel that music shouldn't be studied as a science, but naturally used like art. And other than learning some basics, they don't go on to master advanced principles of music theory, scales, harmony, etc. But on the other hand, many musicians feel that music should be studied and that learning advanced musical knowledge opens up a world of possibilities. If you agree with the second group, then this chapter is indeed very important. It will teach you scientifically proven facts of how the mind learns new information and ways to dramatically improve your learning potential.

What we'll do in this chapter is learn how to learn. As strange as that may sound there are definite procedures for studying and memorizing information effectively. As any college student will tell you, study skills and habits will make all the difference when it comes to how well you can understand and learn information. Using the right techniques can reduce the time of learning a particular textbook chapter (as an example) from 10 hours down to 5 or 6 hours, as well as improve how well the information is memorized and understood. These methods are well known and have been used for decades by college students and researchers. They are mostly based on principles of psychology and brain function. You may recognize many principles from other chapters in this book.

This chapter should be used in conjunction with the memory chapter and the information from either chapter can be used in combination with the other. The basic difference between this chapter and the chapter on memory is that the memory techniques are mostly designed for memorizing information (songs, lyrics, theory) whereas this chapter is designed for developing an understanding of a concept, i.e. understanding harmonic sequences for the purpose of arrangement skills. Learning usually requires memory, but memory doesn't always require learning. You can memorize a song, and there's nothing needed to learn, but learning how to construct chords, for example, requires the memorizing of formulas (i.e. the major seventh chord is constructed: root, 3rd, 5th, maj 7th.), as well as understanding the process.

The debate over whether it's truly important to study music theory has been going on for years, and it's really up to you to decide if it's worth the time and effort to learn the mechanics of music. Not every musician is interested in learning advanced music theory. Many great musicians can play amazing songs and solos, and they yet can't describe in musical terms what they are doing. Their fingers know where to go, but they couldn't tell you why they are choosing certain notes other than that it sounded good. But this I will say, once I learned theory it opened up a lot of options for my songwriting, and I can only compare it to a painter who has more colors to choose from. Sure a painter can still do amazing things with just five different colors but give him 20 colors to choose from and his paintings can achieve deeper levels of expression.

The most significant (and amazing) thing about learning is that when the mind develops a new understanding of a concept, whether it is how to multiply numbers or fix a carburetor, the brain releases certain chemicals that stimulate the pleasure senses. This means that you are rewarded with a small mental and physical rush when you learn something new. It is nature's way of increasing our likelihood of survival. We've all heard the old saying "knowledge is power". Well, power is survival and the number one instinct we humans have is survival. Therefore, we are rewarded when we gain knowledge as an automatic survival mechanism. You may not have sensed this little rush, especially compared to the types of artificial stimulation we have become accustomed to (alcohol, caffeine, etc.), but the next time you are trying to figure something out, and finally say to yourself " Wow! I finally get it" ("Eureka"), take notice of how you feel. You'll definitely notice a physical high and a sudden elevation in your mood, energy, and senses. And even if this little "rush" doesn't seem like that colossal of a high, your subconscious thinks it is and is noticing the reward. The reason I mention this first is that by being aware of an actual chemical change in your body when you learn something, you will have a better appreciation of the physical aspect (on an electro-chemical level) of how the brain functions and the techniques that follow will make more sense.

So now that you realize nature is on our side when it comes to learning, we can take things a step further and do what we humans do best, tamper with nature for our own gain. As crude as that may sound, there's nothing wrong with developing certain improvements or adjustments to nature. Otherwise, curing disease would be considered wrong. And anyway, it's human nature to try to change nature for our own improved survival.

Now let's look at some other facts about how we learn. As promised before, I won't turn this into a biology lesson. I've been trying to keep the scientific history behind these improvement techniques to a minimum. However, sometimes a certain amount of background knowledge will help us understand the big picture, which then helps you apply all this to your musical improvement. It's been proven that the average person only uses about ten percent of their brain. That even includes the subconscious. We don't know why this is, but maybe it leaves room for evolution. Regardless, there's no limit to how much information we can store. Some people feel that by achieving too much information, they can clutter the mind and will forget things that they learned before. That just isn't true. There's no limit to the information the human mind can hold. Scientists have suggested that if you wanted to, and spent all of your time studying, you could learn and memo-rize every book in a large library. Maybe not word for word but the overall information. So don't worry that in order to learn large amounts of information, you may lose some things that you've already learned.

When you study information, it is first put into short-term memory. Short-term memory is not very deeply implanted and is easily forgotten. For information to become permanently learned, it must be stored in the mind's long-term memory. For information to make the switch from short-term to long-term, certain chemical reactions must take place in the brain. Certain proteins are synthesized, oxygen levels are boosted, and the blood flow to specific parts of the brain is increased. All this cre-ates new nerve pathways and chemical triggers that is the basis for storing information.

The difference between memorizing a phone number and memorizing how a flashlight works is that the phone number is a simple sequence of numbers and doesn't require anything but simple memory (even if it's long-term). But memorizing how a flashlight works requires the information to coordinate with information already stored in other parts of the brain, such as: what a battery is and how it works, basic principles of electricity, how a light bulb converts electricity into light, etc. This is the difference between just memorizing some information and learning what something is or how something works. Learning requires coordination with information stored elsewhere in the brain.

Let's put these two principles to work. First- the brain goes through chemical changes in order to permanently store information. Second- the brain has to coordinate the new information with previously learned information. For these chemical changes to take place, it's best to take small breaks now and then while studying. It's during the breaks that the brain can rest a little and get to work making the chemical changes to store the new information. The more relaxing the rest is, the better. A mini meditation session (5 to 10 minutes) is a great way to do this.

Another way to improve the brain's chemical function during the learning process, and specifically the increased need for oxygen in the blood, is to develop deep and rhythmic breathing. It's been pointed out that most people, due to stress or poor habit, take shallow breaths and don't receive the proper amount of air into the lungs. This in turn reduces the amount of oxygen in the blood. Simply put, breathing delivers oxygen to the bloodstream, and then to the brain. The correct balance of oxygen in the brain's overall chemical makeup has a lot to do with how well it functions. So not only does rhythmic breathing relax you, which helps the brain to establish an optimal wave frequency, but it also increases the level of oxygen in the brain which directly improves how well it operates.

Once again, here's an example of a subject that can be applied to a number of different chapters, and just like meditation and self-hypnosis, breathing has wide-spread benefits for musicians. Apply proper breathing techniques to overcoming stage fright, improving concentration, sharpening your memory, improving dexterity, and even enhancing your creativity. Remember, the brain and nervous system are fueled by oxygen, and a system that isn't receiving enough fuel will run at a weaker and slower level.

Third- to improve the brain's ability to coordinate its different parts, thus optimizing the learning process, meditation once again is used. You've probably concluded by now that meditation, with all the ways it improves brain function, is probably one of the best things a musician can do. I would definitely agree with that. Mediation, because it improves inter-brain coordination, helps to merge the left and right hemispheres and their related functions. To summarize once again, the right hemisphere controls logic and analytical reasoning, while the left hemisphere controls creative expression and artistic appreciation. As any musician knows, music is not only mathematical patterns and computations but also expression and imagination. When it comes to the study of music, it's best to have all these aspects coordinated in order to truly develop an understanding of the subject. So meditation once again is a tool used to improve brain function in a way that directly affects musical skill.

Another way to improve learning is based on the fact that the brain works on a certain pulse or rhythm. To summarize how brain rhythms work, when you are asleep or relaxed, the brain's pulse is slow, and when you are very alert and active, the brain has a much quicker pulse. Studies have shown that the brain functions better when it is operating at a slow to medium pulse. This fact can be taken advantage of and applied to learning. The more relaxed you are when you are studying, the better the brain will absorb information. It helps make the electro-chemical changes necessary and permanently stores the information. It is easy to use this information to improve your studying. Simply get into a relaxed state before the study session. This can be done with slow, deep breathing, a quick meditation session, a hot bath or Jacuzzi, or whatever means you find easiest.

Another very common study technique is to play certain types of music in the background while you study. Studies have shown that some songs, because of their tempo and overall rhythm, will put the brain into an optimum rhythm for deep mental activity. The following is a list of classical music pieces that are known to achieve just such a mental rhythm. They are far from being the only musical pieces that have this specific rhythm, but researchers have commonly used them for years to achieve slower brain waves. I have chosen some pieces by Bach for these specific examples.

> Largo from concerto in Gmin
> Largo from harpsichord concerto in F min (Aria/ Goldenberg variation)
> Largo from harpsichord concerto in G min
> Corelli: Sarabanda from concerto no 7 in D min
> Preludio (largo) and Sarabanda from concerto in E min
> Preludio (largo) from concerto no 9 in A maj
> Sarabando (largo) from concerto no 10 in F maj.
> Handel: Largo from Concerto no 1 in F (from "Music for the Royal Fireworks")
> Largo from Concerto no 3 in D (from "Music for the Royal Fireworks")
> Largo from Concerto no 1 in B flat at maj op 3

Telemann: Largo from "Double Fantasia" in G Maj for harpsichord

Largo from Concerto in G Maj for viola and strings

Vivaldi: Largo from "Winter"(part 4 of "The Four Seasons")

Largo from Concerto in D mag for guitar and strings

Largo from Concerto in C Maj for mandolin, strings, and harpsichord

Largo from Concerto in D min for viola and harpsichord

Largo from Concerto in F Maj for viola and horns

It might be assumed that any slow moving music or classical music, in general, will achieve the result of slower brain waves. However, the above songs have a unique combination of the pulse, rhythm, tempo, arrangement and other aspects that have been determined to put the brain into a deep and slow state. If you want to expand on these songs, there are places where you can find music that has this specific effect. Here's a partial list of websites that deal with this specific subject. Some have CDs for sale that has carefully selected or composed music that achieves the brain rhythm we've just discussed. Further searching will uncover many other sources for this type of "mind music."

http://www.epub.org.br/cm/n15/mente/musica.html

http://www.twinblues.com/irv.htm

http://www.awakenedminds.com/

http://www.soundhealthseries.com/shs_shscom.asp

It's ironic that music can improve the mind's ability to learn about creating music. But then again, most things in life come full circle.

Another way to achieve slower brain waves is to purchase a brainwave generator. The one that I have is a software program that lets you choose the specific mental characteristics that you want to achieve (deep focus, total relaxation, heightened awareness, etc.). It then plays a repeating sound wave that creates the requested subliminal effect. This program is shareware and can be found at http://www.bwgen.com. There are also cassettes or CDs that play sound waves (not music) for creating certain mental states. The main difference between music and sound waves is which you would rather listen to. Some people may find it annoying to listen to a constant sound wave for an extended period of time, but other people might prefer it to slow and hypnotic sounding music.

Other than music or sound waves, there's also light pulses. But whether it is a metronome set to a specific tempo or a strobe light that pulses to a certain rhythm, the brain will naturally begin to follow a pulse of any origin if it is played long enough. It's indeed a great scientific breakthrough to be able to create a mental state at will by subjecting yourself to audio or visual pulses. This new science can also be applied to increasing your ability to learn.

We have established that a relaxed slowly pulsed mind is the best state to be in when studying, so it should be of no surprise that stress and tension would greatly reduce the mind's ability to learn. As a musician, stress and tension limit our playing, performance, concentration, memory, and now we even find it interfering with our knowledge of music by decreasing our ability to learn new information. If there's one overall enemy of the musician, it is defiantly stress. The pursuit of relaxation is probably one of the most universal tools for those attempting to strengthen their musical abilities.

Another aspect of learning that has been studied is the effect of emotions. It has been shown that emotional turmoil, or just a mild case of the blues, will dramatically decrease the brain's ability to learn. The principle reason for this is that emotional stress leads to excessive thinking, which then blocks our concentration. Concentration is obviously very important for the ability to study (and therefore the chapter on concentration should also be applied to the subject of learning). It's also well known that emotional issues can lead to stress and fatigue, both of which can interfere with learning skills.

While we're on the subject of mental issues and how they affect your ability to learn, another proven fact is that positive self-image seems to directly boost your learning potential. There are a lot of reasons for this, but it all comes down to the fact that learning is an ability similar to playing an instrument. As we've read in the chapter on confidence, self-image is created gradually by implanting positive or negative thoughts. And just as a professional hypnotist can make you believe you are a dog, you can over time hypnotize yourself into believing that you can or can't do certain things. If you occasionally say things to yourself like "I'll never figure this out," "This is too complex, I can't learn this", or "I'm not that smart. I have trouble learning some things", then your mind will act accordingly. Hypnotists have actually convinced subjects that they can't lift a light chair, and when they try, sure enough, they can't lift a chair that they ordinarily could lift with one hand. The mind controls the arm muscles, and the result is that you can't do something if your mind tells you that it can't be done. This applies to all aspects of life. You must correct your brain's programming regarding what it can and can't do. In our case here, you have to re-program your mind that you are capable of learning any knowledge documented by mankind.

Now let's deal with some specific study methods that have been shown to improve your ability to learn. It has been proven that the brain will cycle through different levels of energy when you engage in focused mental activity. Once you begin studying or concentrating, the brain functions strongly for 50 to 60 minutes; then it begins to decrease in energy until it gets a rest. Research has shown that just a 5 to 10-minute break is sufficient to allow the brain to again resume full activity. But rather than use a stopwatch to plan your studying, just keep in mind that you need about a ten-minute break once an hour to maximize the brain's electrochemical cycle. By following this pattern, you can optimize your study time and get a lot more out of every hour of work.

Also regarding timing there are certain times when the brain absorbs information best. These are: in the afternoon, after any kind of rest (relaxation or nap) and an hour after eating (no sooner).

A common practice that many people resort to is cramming. This is usually a last minute act of desperation that comes about because of not giving yourself enough time to study for a test (or learning a song before a gig). Not only is last minute cramming stressful (which interferes with optimal brain function), but it's also been proven that several short study sessions are far better than one very long session. This has a lot to do with the brain's cycles discussed earlier.

Diet and nutritional supplements will also affect the mind's ability to learn. In previous chapters, we outlined various vitamins, foods, minerals, supplements, and pharmaceutical drugs that improve brain function, clarity, memory, and intelligence. These can have obvious effects on our ability to learn. In fact, the entire chapter on memory should be applied to learning and study skills. On a neurological level, memory and learning are semi-related to the same brain functions and nervous system activity.

Here's a quick summary of techniques listed in the memory chapter that can be applied to studying. First, always review information an hour after the initial study session, then again 24 hours later. This reviewing of information will send electrical stimulation to the newly created pathways in the brain, strengthening and reinforcing them. Second, never proceed if you come across a section of information that you don't fully understand. You may think it's OK to pass over a certain part of what you're studying, but many times that bit of information will have an effect on what follows, which can then throw off your understanding of large sections of the subject. It's best to stop and do whatever it takes to clarify anything you are unsure of. Then, and only then, proceed.

We also discussed little tricks like saying certain key bits of information out loud which will increase the number of senses (in this case hearing) being used to stimulate the memory. Then there was the act of making acronyms out of a list of items, like "Excellent Beginning Guitarists Don't Allow Errors" which can stand for the open string notes of a guitar (E, B, G, D, A, E). You can create acronyms for dozens of things, like rules of harmony, chord inversions, modes, etc. And don't forget the trick for memorizing things by walking around the house and associating information with different locations. There are many other memory tips that were discussed, so it is a wise idea to review the memory chapter.

As with the other aspects of mind power, improving learning potential takes time and effort. You can't expect to dramatically improve your mind power a few hours after applying these methods (although many of them will have instant results). Overall, simply incorporate these techniques into your routine then just keep working on them. Many improvements will take place in a day or two while others may take a few weeks or longer. The key is persistence.

6
Creativity

WITHOUT CREATIVITY, THERE would be no music. The whole concept of arranging sounds so that individual pitches create a pleasant sounding combination is by nature very creative. And rhythm, which is the combination of beats and timing, is also the creation of the human imagination. These arrangements of notes and rhythms can either sound very pleasing to the ear, or they can annoy you worse than fingernails down a blackboard. The ability alone to combine musical elements into a song isn't enough to be considered creative. The musical phrasing and rhythms have to sound good to a significant number of people, not just you. If you alone feel that your songs are creative masterpieces, yet 99.9% of everyone who hears them think they're horrible, then it could be said that your creative abilities as a songwriter would not be considered good.

Usually, when a beginning songwriter attempts his first song, he is so pleased with being able to write a song at all that it sounds, to his ears, like the greatest composition ever created. But as the creative process develops and experience is gained with combining chords into progressions and progressions into arrangements, the ear then becomes a bit more critical and analytical.

For our purposes here, we will define creativity as not just the ability to create music, but the ability to create music that will stand up to at least a minimal level of musical evaluation. After all, even someone who just picked up a guitar five minutes ago may be able to write a crude song, so we have to define creativity within a certain range of quality. And if you are trying to enhance your creative abilities, keep in mind that you are trying for at least a basic degree of artistic talent. Anyone can write a simple song, but by developing your creativity to its fullest potential, you can write genuine masterpieces.

Let's first look into the mental process that gives us the ability to create something. Webster defines creativity as – "Productive originality: Characterized by originality and expressiveness; Productive; creating; Having the ability or power to create". These definitions focus on the words: original, produce, express, and create. First of all, true creativity is the ability to make something totally original, from scratch, without any existing foundation. If you take an existing song and change it around, even if it sounds very different from the original, you still are using someone else's foundation. True creativity is the ability to start with absolutely nothing and to produce something totally new. Although it still may be clever to change an existing song around, and there's creative talent necessary to do it, you aren't reaching down to the level of deep sub-consciousness to create from within.

Another definition was expressiveness. The very act of creating music is an expression of your personality, emotions, and tastes. Always be true to who you are when composing, and you will achieve deeper levels of creativity. What mental process ignites that first spark of inspiration when you create something totally new? On a mental level, creativity involves brain signals traveling through existing networks of neural-chemical connections, choosing bits and pieces of existing information, and combining them into new pathways.

If you compose a melody that goes something like: C, D#, F G, the memories and overall knowledge of those notes already exist. You are taking these notes and creating a totally new signal path by connecting them together. Even if you are sitting at a piano and are just playing random notes until something sounds good, you are still using your brain's network of memories by realizing that you've stumbled across something new. Regardless of which method you use to write songs, the brain must first access existing memories, emotions and established skills in order to make the new pathways needed to create something new. It's hard to compose a song with a trumpet unless you already have the skill to play it.

What makes certain people more creative than others? Let's start with the overall description of the average creative person. It's been said that very creative people have uncommon thought patterns. Their thinking is very haphazard and flowing compared to the average person who's thought patterns are more structured and organized. For example, the average person thinks of the fact that they have to stop at the store and pick up milk. They then think: first -when it would be best to do it (imagining the days schedule and visualizing doing it after work). Second - the route to the store and how it can be done en route from their work to their home. Third - other things that they may also need as long as they're at the store. Fourth - the cost of the item or items and whether they have enough money on them. Fifth - other little specific things, like the brand of milk (if they have a preference).

You may not realize that all these thoughts are going through your mind regarding such a small task, but for everything you plan or think about, a huge amount of mental activity takes place. Usually, you aren't even aware of all these thoughts because they've become very automatic and unnoticed. But whether you notice you're thinking or not, we all have certain thought patterns and overall mental habits regarding how we organize our thoughts.

For the very creative person, however, it has been determined that their thought habits are a lot different than average. Regarding the example of buying milk at the store, they probably will think of all of the things's the average person would (when, where, how, and cost) but in addition to these basic thoughts they tend to go a little deeper into the overall subject. They may think additional thoughts such as they might meet someone at the store such as a certain checkout clerk they're attracted to. Then maybe in the future, they can buy gallons instead of just quarts to save numerous trips to the store. Also the fact that drinking milk is good for them, so even this small trip to buy milk is contributing to their health. Then possibly they'll try something different, such as buying chocolate milk for a change, etc.

The point I'm making is that they tend to think more thoughts and on deeper levels than the average person. All of this thinking requires electrochemical activity and sending signals through many combinations of neurological pathways. And in addition to more thoughts, they use a unique order of thoughts that aren't always in logical sequence. For example, they might first visualize someone they'll meet at the store before thinking about the actual purchase of the milk. As I mentioned, all these thoughts are so quick and automatic, that you probably don't even notice them. It's only after analyzing your mental reaction to common activities that you can become aware of your thought patterns.

All of this may not seem relevant to the subject of enhancing your musical creativity but it demonstrates your mind's operating habits, and when you learn new mental habits you can greatly improve your creativity. The brain's ability to send signals through new paths and connections is the result of trying new ways of thinking, and when brain signals travel new paths, new possibilities become apparent. But how can you put this knowledge to work? I'm certainly not suggesting that you reprogram your entire mentality. The way you think is a large part of who you are, and a big aspect of music is expressing who you are, not changing it. But if you find it difficult to write songs and feel that it's important enough to make some changes to improve your creativity, then a few mental habits can go a long way.

First of all, try to think at a deeper level. Many people feel that efficient, streamlined thinking is important and that it will benefit them overall in life. For accountants and other analytical professions, this may be true. But creativity requires the mind to go into deeper levels of thought that may not always seem logical. If you think about it, daydreaming is not a logical habit and serves no practical purpose. But the act of allowing your thoughts to wander and invent images, stories, scenarios, and situations is a prime example of deep thinking.

All this doesn't mean that you have to completely overhaul your mental habits. Just add a new aspect to your thinking. Think of the "behind the scenes" aspects of everyday things. When you buy a new CD, before you even play it for the first time, imagine the whole chain of events that led to you buying this CD.

Think of the songwriters who crafted the music, the engineers who recorded it at the recording studio, the record company executives who ironed out all the logistics of promotion, costs, production, and distribution, and even the shipment of the CDs to stores around the country. Allow yourself to take in " the big picture" behind everyday things. Overall, think more often and on deeper levels. Don't take this to unhealthy excessiveness, as do some people who have overactive minds and think all the time. This can lead to an unbalanced mind. As with everything in life: moderation rules. Simply add a controlled amount and depth of thought to your everyday life. Later in this chapter, we'll discuss many other techniques for specifically sharpening your creative powers, but the ability to think on deeper levels definitely comes first and is the prerequisite for all other creativity boosters.

Another mental habit that will improve overall creativity is positive thinking. A negative image of your creativity is a huge block to the mind's ability to create. This is very similar to how a negative self-image of your performance skills leads to stage fright and limits your ability to play in front of an audience. If you haven't already read the chapter on confidence, you'll see how important positive thinking is to the brain's ability to function and perform specific skills.

You should be aware that creativity, just like any other skill, can be either boosted or limited by self-hypnotism, whether it is gradual and unintentional or specifically planned sessions. The most common beginning to a negative self-image with regard to creativity is when you try to compose your first song or two and are unhappy with the results. This starts the ball rolling that makes you feel that your musical creativity is lacking. What usually happens is that instead of realizing that songwriting just takes a little practice, the person concludes that there must be a lack of inner creative talent, otherwise they would have written a decent song. Once this voice of self-doubt is established, it doesn't take long before it interferes with your song-writing concentration. It will begin to block your creative flow and limit your ability to compose a decent song. If this chain of events isn't stopped, the result is a lifetime of unsuccessful composing and the sure belief that you can't write a good song to save your life. However, if you become aware of this mental condition early enough, you can either prevent it from starting, or you can use certain methods to reverse the escalating negative thinking. Rather than go through it all again, refer to the chapter on confidence for techniques on improving self-image, confidence, and positive thinking. Then simply apply these tools to enhancing creativity.

One way to develop creativity is to study the talents and techniques of past composers. By seeing what many great composers had in common, you can then apply these traits to your musical and personal habits. Fortunately for us, much research has been done into the habits and personalities of many of the great composers of the past, such as Chopin, Beethoven, Mozart, and Bach. Sigmund Freud has even posthumously psycho-analyzed some of these great composers in an attempt to find common psychological traits.

A basic summary of these geniuses is as follows: their overall intelligence was very mediocre and average. Apparently great intelligence is not required (or may even interfere) with strong creativity. They seemed to demonstrate certain characteristics of a psychotic personality. Freud concluded that genius composers and psychotics have many mental traits in common. This doesn't mean they were mentally unbalanced but suggests that their mind's random flow of brain signals (which is partly required for creativity) was so intense that their chain of thought seemed strange to many people. They seemed to be loners with a minimum of friends and social contact. If you think about people you know who prefer to be alone, they are often engaged in deep thought. They were very emotional, quick to anger, cry, or become thrilled. They were all very mathematically gifted, were problem solvers and enjoyed puzzles or figuring out problems, mysteries or dilemmas. They also had great faith in their creative abilities. As an example, they felt no fear in waiting until the last minute to finish composing an opera that had a deadline. They weren't worried that they might have a creative slump or that they wouldn't be able to finish the composition in time. They fully believed in their creativity. They had very large egos and had very positive self-images. They didn't fear criticism, nor let it shake their confidence. Criticism usually angered them, but it never intimidated them. They possessed rebelliousness towards established standards, especially music. Many of them even wrote their own rules of musical theory, scales, and harmonic structures.

I'm sure I don't need to summarize these behaviors and mental traits. They're very obvious. Either you already possess some of these traits, or, if your quest for creativity is important enough to you, you can try to incorporate them into your overall way of thinking. For example, being more in touch with your emotions is one attribute that you can work on. Some qualities could be achieved by simply allowing your mind to be more flexible, imaginative, and active. Simply develop certain mental habits that would expand your mind's ability to invent and create.

Some of the negative traits that were listed, such as borderline psychotic behavior, would be unwise to try to develop - obviously. I'm certianly not suggesting that you deliberately become mentally unbalanced for the sake of improving your songwriting skills. It just so happens that psychotic personalities and creative geniuses have some similar thought patterns, usually regarding increased brain activity and neurological signals traveling into more and deeper regions of the brain. There's an old maxim that states, "Genius is a form of madness". However, despite this comparison between creativity and unbalanced thinking, the creative person still has control over his or her mind, whereas the psychotic does not. Moderation is very important here.

There are other aspects of behavior and personality common to many great composers - such as exhibiting rebellious behavior and avoiding social contact, but these are usually very deep-rooted personality traits. If you don't already possess them, I certainly again wouldn't suggest trying to change your whole personality. However, certain harmless traits that help with creativity might be beneficial to incorporate into an overall approach to songwriting.

Let's focus more on emotions. If you feel that you tend to be slightly thick skinned or shallow, then trying to get in touch with your emotions might be a good way to enhance your creativity. This can be achieved by becoming more aware of how things make you feel, like when watching something sad on TV. Try to put yourself into the inner feeling of the situation. If it's a movie where the hero's love is killed (wife, girlfriend, boyfriend, etc.), reach down and try to experience what it would feel like if it happened to you.

Remember past events of intense sadness and feel that emotion. Always make sure you have control over these emotions. For some people, the problem is that they are too in touch with emotions, which can be mentally unhealthy. But if you have trouble getting in touch with your inner feelings, then making an effort to develop this ability will add great depth to your compositions.

Your mind is usually very open to deep levels when you are experiencing intense emotions. If you think about it, an entire genre of music is based on emotions; it's called the Blues. It's even been said that unless you've experienced pain in your life, you'll never become a great writer. Whether or not this is true, it's still agreed on by most composers that your best material can be written during emotional episodes. This doesn't have to always mean sad times either. Whether your lover has just left, you or you just won the lottery, make it a point to use that emotional energy to write with. However, as previously mentioned, never let emotions become overwhelming or let them block other needed aspects of your mind power, such as concentration.

Also, find the child in yourself. As children, we were very open to deeper levels of consciousness. For example, when was the last time you jumped up and down because it was your birthday? Chances are it was when you were nine or ten years old. As we grow older, we learn to control and bury our feelings. But as a writer, we should try to uncover those feelings again. This will affect more than just your ability to express feelings; it will also allow you to overcome the adult habit of maintaining the mature composure that we think is important, especially around other adults. Let loose and create, even if it's something silly, illogical, or absurd. By holding back, you are stifling your creativity. Stop taking yourself so seriously and start composing whatever comes to mind. You don't have to show anybody everything you come up with, remove the self-consciousness when it's time to write songs.

Other than adapting yourself to common personal traits of creative people, there are many other techniques for enhancing creativity and songwriting. The following are some common creativity boosters. Not all these things will appeal to you, but some of these techniques and habits might prove valuable to your overall composing skills.

Many songwriters feel that listening to the radio or CD's of other people's music clouds their mind with musical phrases, and this interferes with their ability to come up with new and original material. For example, have you ever had a melody or riff from a certain song stuck in your mind and found that when you tried to write, that melody kept popping up? Beethoven made it a point never to go to concerts given by any of his colleagues. He felt that it would contaminate his creativity. You may find it hard or overly obsessive not to listen to the radio, go to concerts, or play CD's, but maybe you can at least compromise. Try not to listen to music on certain days when you plan on writing. This will keep your mind fresh and clear of other melodies and riffs.

As mentioned in other chapters, the mind functions at different speeds or frequencies. It's been well-established that the slowest brain frequency, known as the thera state, allows us to access deep levels of consciousness and enables intense creativity. There's a number of ways to utilize the thera state. When you first wake up or when you are about to drift off to sleep are good times to compose music, but make sure to record yourself because it might be hard to remember what you wrote later in the day. Because these times only occur twice a day, you can also achieve this twilight state by purposely initiating it. This can be accomplished by either taking naps or entering the relaxed thera state, as when you prepare for self-hypnosis (as detailed in the motivation chapter). You should prepare for these sessions by having your instrument and a tape recorder nearby.

Apply the techniques in the concentration chapter to songwriting sessions. Sharpen your focus to the point of being able to block out all outside distractions. By utilizing super concentration and other elements of mind power gained through meditation and self-hypnosis, you can reach down to levels of consciousness and emotion that you ordinarily wouldn't be able to achieve. It's said that true inspiration can only be realized by focusing the mind to very deep levels. As with many skills learned in this book, this will take some work.

Practice creativity building exercises, such as puzzles and word games. Make it a point to read books as opposed to watching TV. The act of reading requires you to visualize things, like the faces of the characters, the scenery, etc. This is a very creative act. When you watch TV, this is all done for you and the mind has nothing to do except to take it all in.

Practice composing music in your mind. Most songwriters will use their instrument to experiment with riffs and chord progressions until they stumble across something that they think has potential. Instead of using your instrument to compose, try doing it mentally. Many of the great composers of the past did this when they composed very complex symphonies and operas. You don't have to replace your usual method of composing but occasionally use mental songwriting in addition to it.

One of the advantages of this method is that it can be done anywhere, anytime. Next time you're in a traffic jam compose a melody in your mind. Do this even if just as a means of practicing your creativity. If you find that this works well for you, you can begin to use it as one of your regular tools for composing. To be on the safe side use a small handheld tape recorder or your cell phone in case you do come up with a killer melody.

The above habits, over time, or in some cases right away, will improve your songwriting ability. But the best way to develop songwriting is to write songs, hundreds of them. It's by far the best way to develop your "chops" as they say. Also, you will find a distinct style emerging over time. Your personal style of songwriting is a combination of influences and preferences, but also of hooks, phrasing, and melodic nuances. Your influences and musical preferences already exist and have been created over your lifetime. But your phrasing and the use of harmony and melody will take time to truly develop into a style that only you can create. We've all heard songs that only after a few notes or phrases we know who wrote it. Just as certain people have individual ways of speaking, most composers have a signature style, and the songs they write will have a certain musical personality unique to that composer.

Don't feel that every song you write has to be polished or even recorded. Just for practice, try to write at least one song a day without bothering to write it down or record it (unless you come up with something really good, of course). Experiment with new scales, strange chords, and unique harmonies. Sometimes you have to rule many things out before you arrive at something that works.

One aspect of composing that many people disagree over is the importance of music theory. One school of thought is that to truly have a full arsenal to work with, you should be well versed in scales, chords, harmonic structure and all other elements of musical knowledge. These people feel that just as a painter needs many different colors to paint with, a musician needs knowledge to truly create. Their attitude is that without knowing the rules of harmony, a composer is only guessing at ways to create a well-balanced musical structure.

The other school of thought is that music is based on the ear and that one does not need to know why or how something works in order to create a good sounding song. These people point to certain well-known songwriters who knew nothing about musical theory yet composed some of the world's greatest songs. According to these people, the only reason that the rules of musical structure even exist is to explain why things sound good to the ear and not the other way around. In that case, the only thing that matters is that you know what makes sense to your ears and that memorizing a bunch of rules takes the spirit out of music and is a waste of time. Personally, I think there's truth in both these views. Many of the songs that I've written were composed by ear without any concern for rules of harmonic structure, key modulation, scales or any other aspects of music theory. However, I've also written a few tunes that were intense and harmonically interesting (in my humble opinion) and consisted of an interconnected series of chords that followed the rules of harmonic progression. These songs would have been very difficult if not impossible; to create by ear alone and it was only because I knew my scales and rules of harmony that I was able to build something very complex with relative ease.

Another aspect of songwriting is learning a composition system. Most songwriters use one system or another, even if they're not aware that they're doing so. For example, some composers establish the melody first then find chords that fit. Other songwriters do just the opposite. They write a chord progression first then they write a melody that works. Then there's the use of intervals, which implies arranging chords (or melody notes) in sequences that follow a scale. For example, if a scale has seven notes, then choosing notes 1, 4 and 5 (which is a common arrangement) creates a sequence. We can go a lot deeper into the art of musical arrangement, but that's subject for another book. The point I'm making is that songwriting can be aided by having a certain formula (or formulas) you can rely on. Even creativity can be organized.

If the thought of spending time and effort learning music theory bothers you, yet you agree that it can be a major benefit to your songwriting, then perhaps the chapters on motivation and learning can help. First, get psyched, roll up your sleeves and become determined to face the challenge. Then apply some study techniques that will make the process quicker and more efficient. You'll thank yourself in the end, especially when it comes to composing.

Meditation and self-hypnosis are also valuable tools for the development of creativity. Meditation is known to build a stronger coordination between the left and right hemispheres of the brain, as well as other regions. This improved mental network has a direct effect on creativity. As we mentioned before, the left hemisphere controls technical reasoning, and the right hemisphere controls the emotional aspects of thought and the appreciation of beauty. Being that music is a calculated and mathematical combination of notes and sequences, as well as an artistic expression of emotion, both hemispheres come into play. The better these two halves coordinate, the better you will be able to write songs.

Meditation also puts us into the thera state, and as previously pointed out this mental state allows us to reach very deeply into the mind. By routinely practicing meditation we can gradually create easier access to deeper levels of consciousness. This opens up a strong flow of creativity. You can also develop a routine of composing right after awakening from meditation and take immediate advantage of this mental condition.

And once again the act of self-hypnosis is a great tool for the musician. Self-hypnosis is a very useful and direct way to implant creative abilities and habits into the subconscious. We've already discussed the process of self-hypnosis in other chapters, so there's no need to run through it again. However, you need to know a few specific things to implant into the subconscious. It may or may not be effective to simply tell the subconscious "I am a very creative person." This is probably too vague for the mind to act on and as I mentioned before the more specific you are with your implants, the more effective they will be.

Here's a brief list to get you started. You can come up with your own sentences as desired or create your own using these as guidelines.

"I can create very strong and expressive melodies."

"I can come up with very interesting and unique chord progressions."

"I can utilize my knowledge of music theory to write creative and interesting songs."

"I can develop a very individual style of composing that is new and different."

"I have a great love for composing and am willing to work very hard at writing songs."

Self-hypnosis can help build creativity on a subconscious level. The thing about creativity is that it is both a mental trait as well as a conscious skill. We all possess a certain amount of creativity, and although songwriting does become easier with practice, it is also possible to improve creative ability by establishing certain subconscious links. This subject is indeed a perfect example of how mind power can be harnessed to achieve an accelerated talent that we can apply to music.

Musical creativity definitely can be acquired fairly quickly if you use the right tools to do it. Below are the tools needed to enhance your creative abilities and song-writing skills:

Believe deep down that you have the ability to write great songs.

Improve the musical skills and knowledge that will arm you with the required tools for composing.

Use specific techniques for developing and improving the mental flow of ideas, such as: composing when you first wake up, composing right after meditation

Avoiding listening to the radio or CDs before composing.

Develop overall creative habits and ways of thinking.

Be more open to your inner emotions.

Experiment with songwriting systems.

Practice writing songs as often as possible.

Find the child in yourself and let loose with your songwriting.

Remember creativity isn't a genetic trait like your eye color or metabolism. It can be enhanced.

7
Concentration

IN THIS CHAPTER, we'll discuss ways to improve concentration, a very important element for any musician. Concentration is relatively self-explanatory and is a mental component that many people need to improve upon. A weak concentration can lead to losing track while playing a song, difficulty following a progression, forgetting which scale you're playing from, falling out of tempo, and many other problems.

Mental dullness and the lack of concentration are sometimes associated with low I.Q. However, it can merely be a habit that has been developed – one of mental laziness. It is the inability to focus on things that you are doing or that you are trying to learn - such as music theory or a song's arrangement. It can also just be an overall mental fog that we sometimes feel. This is common as we all have those days when we have trouble making sense of things.

An example of this is when someone asks you for your phone number, and you need time to think of it, or when you are doing a simple math problem, and it takes a lot longer then you know it should.

Many people think of these mental characteristics as being a part of your natural born mentality and therefore can't be improved upon. Some think it's a permanent part of their biology, like their height or eye color. The basic theme of this book is that mental sharpness can be improved. This issue has been so thoroughly proven by science and research that's it's no longer even debated. Every psychologist, neurologist, physician, and teacher knows that mind power can be improved with effort. Through certain procedures, you can sharpen your concentration and strengthen your overall mental proficiency. While researching for this book I came across numerous books and articles confirming this fact.

I'm not going to claim that the potential for mental improvement is unlimited. There are ofcourse the conditions of mental retardation, brain damage, or other physical limitations that medical science has yet to overcome. But if you know that you're just an average healthy person, then your degree of mental growth will mostly be dependent on the amount of work you put into it.

It has been said that average humans use only about 10% of the brain's potential. There are many reported cases of stroke victims, whose brains have been badly damaged, learning how to activate other unused sections of their brain to regain speech, coordination, and other abilities. Moreover, there are countless success stories of people who decided that they were tired of being mentally sluggish, and who worked to achieve stronger memories and better concentration. Much of this is based on the same principles that describe why one's fingers can become lightning-fast and accurate on the guitar or piano after years of practice. It's simply the electrochemical activation of neurons that create an engraved path through the brain and nervous system.

What I'm going to do in this chapter is list and describe various techniques for improving your mind's focus and sharpness. And although we may be dealing with improving your mind's sharpness, you also have to work on improving *your* sharpness. My point is that it takes more than just exercises designed to improve brain function. You still need to improve personal habits such as laziness, indifference, stubbornness, and the lack of motivation.

As I've mentioned, one of the leading causes of mental sluggishness in people is that they are just plain mentally lazy. Whether it's due to fatigue or personality, if you don't make the effort or even care about focusing your mind, then you will be mentally unfocused. Before we begin the different techniques for sharpening the mind, take the time to honestly ask yourself if you aren't just somewhat lazy when it comes to focusing, figuring things out, memorizing, and/or learning new things. Then before applying the methods discussed in this chapter (and future chapters), take personal steps to apply yourself more. Motivate yourself (read the chapter on motivation) to elicit the needed effort to be more mentally aware and active. Often motivation alone will dramatically result in improved mental clarity and mind-power. If you find it hard to muster the energy to increase mental exertion, then I suggest you look into increasing your energy through a better diet (reducing junk foods and taking vitamins), improving your health habits (getting enough sleep, reducing or quitting drinking and smoking, etc), or seeing a doctor to establish an all-out plan for increasing your energy. I actually thought about including a chapter on energy in this book but decided just to touch on the subject as it applies to each aspect of improvement.

In the chapter on motivation, I mention how motivation must come first or else you won't have the desire to do the work needed to accomplish your musical goals. Energy is just as important because without it we lack the drive and the stamina to make improvements. But since this book is about aspects of the mind, I'll only occasionally mention the physical aspect of energy and its importance with regard to mental improvement.

This chapter will define different ways to improve concentration. The first techniques are some simple "brain-teaser" type exercises that you may have seen in the form of puzzles. They are usually designed for entertainment, but could actually serve as important tools for exercising brain function. The best are the ones that ask you to view information and then tests you to see how much attention you have paid to detail.

One example that comes to mind is an exercise where you are first allowed five minutes to view a simple street map of a small town. Then you are tested with questions like: "If you make a left at the library and go up two streets, what building will be on your right?" This may seem more like a memory test, but as I've pointed out, all of the different aspects of mind power are inter-related. If you had concentrated and paid strict attention to the map, remembering it would have been easy. Memory was explored very thoroughly in the memory chapter.

One example of a book that has numerous brain exercises is " Brain Fitness" by Monique Le Poncin (Fawcett / Columbine - 1990). It's loaded with exercises designed to stimulate and improve a variety of brain functions such as focus, logic, memory, etc. There are many books like this available. Completing these types of brain exercises have been scientifically proven to establish new neuron connections, stimulate electro-chemical activity in new and deeper sections of the brain, and forces the brain to work in ways that create mental growth. Research has shown that older people who suffer from diminished brain function can dramatically benefit from brain exercises to sharpen and improve their minds. I would simply recommend spending ten minutes a day doing one of these specifically designed puzzles to sharpen your concentration. Your other brain functions (ex. memory, logic) will also improve as a result.

I'll give you an example of a focus exercise I invented myself. It is an exercise aimed at blocking out distraction - which is one of the leading limiters of concentration. We all know the child's song "Row, Row Your Boat," that is sung with several voices, all starting their verse at a different time. Once all the voices have joined in the song sounds like total confusion with everyone singing different parts all at once. Each singer is required to concentrate in order to block out the other voices and keep in time with their specific part. I came up with a way to practice blocking out distraction similar to that. Simply play a CD of some music (or the radio but music should be playing) with the volume up fairly loud. Then with your instrument play a song you know without losing track of arrangement, tempo, breaks, etc. It's tough if the tempo of the background music is radically different or if there are a lot of breaks. Another distraction blocking exercise is to simply play in front of a few people and try to totally forget they are there. If you can get good at blocking out the biggest distraction of them all, self-consciousness, you can then kiss stage fright goodbye (we discussed stage fright in the chapter on confidence), and your playing on stage will improve more than what five years of hard practice could achieve. Many of us feel frustrated because when we're alone, we can play great, then ten minutes later if we were to play in front of people –wham! a total reduction of ability. This is because half of our concentration is being taken away from playing and being diverted to the awareness of people watching us. This exercise can be done at small bars on open stage night, family barbecues or any get-together. Try to start with just one or two people, then once you feel that you can play with 100% focus, totally forgetting they are even in the room, move on to bigger crowds progressively. This is probably one of the most important exercises in this book for musicians who want to perform live.

Another way to exercise concentration is to utilize technology. There's been a whole industry developed around electrical devices that stimulate and improve brain function. You simply put one of these devices in your office or bedroom (wherever you'll be spending a lot of time), set the light or sound pulse at a specific tempo, and go about your business. You can also specifically incorporate a device into a meditation or hypnosis session. The concept here is that your brain's natural electrical activity will be stimulated and strengthened by being harmonized with a specific pulse frequency. There are probably hundreds of different devices of this kind on the market varying in the specific targeted brain function, the way it delivers the actual brain stimulation, cost, etc. If this is of interest to you, you can check out a book titled "Mega Brain Power" by Michael Hutchison (1994 Hutchison). In it is listed many devices of this type and techniques for using them. As a musician, I find the science of controlling brain waves with electrical devices to be fascinating. It scientifically shows how we are physically affected by sound and music. The book explores how sound can have a dramatic effect on brain function and even discusses certain types of music as a means of improving the efficiency of the brain's electrical pulses.

Although the previously listed techniques can do wonders for sharpening focus, meditation is by far the most direct, intense, and easiest way to create a super concentration. It gets to the core of the biggest problem affecting concentration - mind noise. The main reason we have trouble focusing is that we are distracted. Most people are aware of external distractions such as a baby crying or a leaking faucet, but these are easy to shut out of your mind once you learn how to deal with the biggest distraction - inner noise.

All of us have a continuous flow of mind activity that we don't control. It's almost as if we can sit back and watch or listen to it like it was coming from somewhere else. It's totally natural; it is the mind at work. It's basically the same mental gears that turn when you dream. It's the never-ending buzz of the mind's computer. It varies from person to person but is mostly a collage of images, sounds, colors, memories, worries, and amusements. It can consist of a quick thought, like a shopping list of what we need to get later, an audio playback of a song we heard on the radio this morning, or a steady stream of colors, movements, and images that are viewed with your "mind's eye."

Without going too far into scientific explanations here is a quick summary of the brain and the effects of meditation on the mind. The brain consists of many different regions, each with its contribution to the brain's overall function. Most obvious is the division into the left and right hemispheres. As already mentioned several times in previous chapters, the left side has been proven to control analytical thought and cold hard logic, and the right side possesses the imaginative and emotional aspects of thought. The anatomy of the brain specifically consists of the cerebellum, the frontal lobe, the basal ganglia, the cerebral cortex, and many other parts. Each part has a specific function. Some parts regulate heart rate, body temperature, and other automatic systems of the body. Some sections deal with motor skills and coordination. Other regions are the center of thought and emotion. In an ideal and perfectly functioning brain, all of these different sections would coordinate together in perfect harmony. However, it has been determined that evolution, diet, environment, and even our cultural habits have created a dysfunction between the different systems and areas of the brain.

One of the most significant benefits of meditation is an equilibrium between the various components of the brain. The cortex having control over motor skills is integrated with the cerebellum and its command of the creative and inspirational aspects of thought. The left hemisphere is unified with the right. Therefore, many other functions are better coordinated. This strengthening of balance has a dramatic effect on the mind. Integration of brain activity is one of the most significant improvements you can make regarding your mind and concentration.

Aside from balancing brain function, meditation is beneficial in a number of other ways. It has the ability to calm brain waves, thus creating the thera wave pattern with its many benefits. The deep relaxation it induces is a way to tone and sharpen the nervous system and brain's electrochemical flow of energy. Meditation also improves hand-eye coordination, increases learning ability, opens access to deep creativity, reduces stress, creates emotional stability, improves self-discipline, and greatly improves concentration. As I've said before, many of the subjects and techniques in this book will have overlapping applications. Mediation has benefits for many different aspects of musical performance, and you will see it mentioned again throughout this book.

So now that we've established that meditation can dramatically sharpen concentration, let's learn how to do it. Much like the procedure for self-hypnosis (motivation chapter), it is best to slow your brain waves down to the thera pulse, which is between 4 to 7 cycles per second. As a reference, the beta brain wave pattern is your basic everyday consciousness. It is between 15 to 25 cycles per second. That pretty well demonstrates the deep level of relaxation that's needed. Adjusting your brain patterns is something that you won't be able to do consciously, but if you learn how to truly relax yourself to the point of feeling weightless, then your brain will naturally slow its pulse. In the motivation chapter, we outlined a method that works well for putting yourself into a deeply relaxed state. However, that technique requires much mental activity and visualization, which is fine for hypnosis because the very act of self-hypnosis requires a lot of mental activity and imagination. But in the case of meditation, the challenge is to quite the mind into absolute stillness and inactivity, so therefore, we should take another approach to relaxation.

The method that I personally have found effective is to consciously slow the breathing, imagine the body being filled with helium, and becoming lighter than air and without using too much mental imagery - just disappearing. Whatever technique you use is fine as long as your body becomes very relaxed and your mind becomes as inactive as possible. Then with your eyes closed and in a location that's free of distraction, sit in a comfortable position either on the floor or in a chair. Try to stop all thoughts from coming into your mind. Become totally aware but totally silent and without thought. If you're like most people, you will find this very hard at first. Try for at least ten minutes but eventually increasing the session to 20 or 30 minutes. The art of meditation might take days to get the hang of, months to become very good at, and years to totally master, but the better you get at it, the more you will experience a very intense "heaven like" feeling.

Aside from the simple technique just listed, an additional step that many people will take is to use what is called a "mantra." This is the use of one, and only one, mental awareness. A mantra is commonly a low hum, a softly repeated word (an old classic is "Ohmmmmm....") or just the awareness of your breathing. Many people find it easier to use a mantra because total nothingness is very difficult to achieve.

When you come out of a very deep session of meditation, your mind has the greatest ability to focus and concentrate that you could ever imagine. It's right after meditation that I like to pick up the guitar and compose, work on difficult pieces, and just take advantage of the intense sharpness that I'm left with. But the effect of meditation isn't just a temporary state that you experience right after a session. With a regular schedule of daily meditation, the effects become a longer lasting part of your mental makeup. You will see major improvements in your ability to concentrate and to shut out distractions which will have positive effects on your musicianship.

Another way to improve concentration is to perform what is known as "walking meditation," which is simply going about your daily business without letting any thoughts come to mind. For example, while driving somewhere try to focus your mind entirely on the road without letting a single thought take over. Simply put, be "here and now", steer the car, watch the road and be aware of any traffic. This is actually very hard to do. You may find it almost impossible to go 30 seconds without having a thought or being mentally distracted from the "here and now" outside world. We all have a habit of letting our minds wander a little when we are doing common everyday things. There is nothing wrong with using your mind to think of memories, review upcoming schedules, or just daydream a little. Actually, it's perfectly natural. But as a concentration exercise occasionally try to practice this intense level of outward focus. Doing this now and then is a great mental workout and can gradually do wonders for your concentration.

A very important subject concerning concentration is emotions. If there's one thing that will distract from your ability to focus, it's emotional turmoil. Your brain seems to take a lot of electrical and chemical resources and devotes them to emotional feelings. It's almost as if emotions take priority over other brain functions. It can be of no surprise that heavy emotions can interfere with your logic and sometimes even survival instincts. You can defiantly do stupid things when clouded by emotions. Only emotions can cause a person to set aside a human's number one instinct, survival, and kill themself. So never underestimate the power of emotions.

Under most conditions, our everyday life isn't affected by emotions. It's usually when a special event or situation happens (falling in love, the death of a loved one, being fired from your job, etc.) that emotions kick into high gear and take over the chemical balance of your brain. Whether it is a good or a bad thing, emotional feelings should be controlled to the point of them not controlling you. It's been proven that you should never bury emotions but deal with them straight on. You have to put a limit on how they are affecting you, or else you end up running red lights, making stupid decisions, and playing your instrument like a musical idiot.

Other than intense emotional stress, we usually just feel a case of the blues (like when our dog dies) or fear (like when we are fired from a job and the rent is due). As a musician, it is difficult to focus and play when we are distracted. Our emotions can do more than just distract; they can highjack the brain's electrical system. So how can we work around this? The following is a list of actions that will regain your musical focus.   First - set aside about an hour and think about your problem - that's right, face it head on. Unless you feel like you've dealt with it, your problem will be nagging you all day long. I usually write down a list of things to correct the problem, or if there's no way to fix the problem, I devise ways of at least controlling the damage or improving the situation. By spending time with the issue, you can mentally resolve some issues, or at least feel like you've got a handle on things. This will allow you to stop constantly thinking about them, which is one of the reasons that emotions interfere with our life. It's the endless thinking which fuels the feelings, which leads to more thinking, which further fuels the emotions, etc. You have to stop this escalating cycle from taking control of your mind or else you can't fully focus while playing your instrument. The first step is to get all that thinking out of your system.

The second step is once you've spent an hour thinking and figuring things out, you then have to stop thinking. Even if you didn't totally resolve the issue, you have to officially put an end to all of the thinking, not just about the emotions but everything. Meditation, as we well know, can quiet our minds. Start with a long meditation session; quiet the mind, then go about your day and make it a point not to think. You will know in the back of your mind that you've already spent a lot of time situating things, and if need be you'll do it again tomorrow- but for now stop thinking. Stopping thought isn't always easy, but if you keep busy and try to focus on real activity, it can be done. As a musician, I don't have to tell you how to keep busy. You have an outlet that many people don't, playing and studying music.

The third step, if the first two steps didn't already work, is to slow the mind down using the pulse generating technology mentioned earlier in this chapter (setting your brain wave rhythm to a slower tempo by using a pulse generator). This along with relaxation techniques should help control the mind so you can steer it away from what's troubling you.

Another way that many people achieve inner peace is with prayer. If it works for you, then by all means do it. For many people, a spiritual balance can steady the nerves and calm the mind. It's indeed an option to keep in mind.

Only after you have a grip on your emotions can you effectively focus on music. If you still are troubled by something (and let's face it, the day after your girlfriend or boyfriend leaves you it's going to be hard sitting down and playing), then just do your best to concentrate on what you're doing and try to get back on your feet as soon as possible.

The subject of emotions is just too complex to fully deal with here. Perhaps you can do some additional research on the Internet. If you truly feel that your emotions are causing you problems, and you are feeling incredibly sad or confused, then you should see a doctor. The mind is no less important than the heart, and if you were feeling severe chest pains, it would be unwise not to see a doctor. The mind is the most complex thing known to mankind, and there's no shame in seeking help from a specialist who has trained many years in the science of mental and emotional conditions. Emotional pain is bad enough don't let it interfere with your music too.

In this chapter, we have established some basic techniques for sharpening concentration and attention span with the use of puzzles, mind exercises, electronic devices, and meditation. We also dealt with the need for energy, good health, emotional stability, fighting mental laziness and overcoming fatigue. If you were to develop your own plan that incorporated all of these elements, it wouldn't take long before you would find your mind as sharp as a razor. You can develop rock solid focus that can push away any distraction allowing you to zero in on the subject of your attention. It doesn't take much to see how this can take your playing to a higher level both directly and by improving the other aspects that are covered in this book such as confidence, memory, dexterity and other keys to musical skill.

8
Mental Sharpness

THE SUBJECT OF mental sharpness is much more vague than the other chapters in this book. Unlike the chapter on confidence for example (which deals with overcoming stage fright), it doesn't focus on just one aspect of a musician's needs, but rather is a general subject that can pertain to many musical situations. I probably could have divided this chapter into a dozen applications, but I felt it best to keep it as an "applies to all" category.

This chapter is probably most closely related to the chapter on concentration. After all, one of the most familiar aspects of overall mind power is the ability to concentrate which consequently leads to higher awareness, better memory, increased understanding, and quicker reflexes and response. However, there are other elements of overall mental sharpness that do not necessarily apply to concentration. They are as follows:

Intelligence - the ability to take in and apply knowledge, logic, and common sense.

Reason - knowing what will result from a certain action,

Learning - the ability to gain an understanding of a subject and to memorize related information,

Intuition - the sense of anticipating how events will turn out in the future or the ability to see situations that are not clearly shown or visible.

Problem-solving - the ability to combine logic and intuition in a way that will overcome obstacles,

Mental quickness - how quickly one can calculate information and/or use any of the above elements,

Emotional control - the ability to act solely on intelligence, not emotion,

Self-discipline - the ability to perform, or refrain from, an action regardless of enjoyment or discomfort.

The accumulated combination of the above mental traits is often what defines a person as intelligent or "sharp-minded". We all know someone who is very quick to answer questions and figure things out. Some people have a very sharp focus and are often the first to see a mistake of some kind or to finish a puzzle. They seem to be able to predict what will happen in a certain situation and are almost always the first to be ready for changes or to react to new developments. We usually think of these people as being mentally gifted or having been born with a powerful mind. But what most people don't realize is that many mental strengths can be acquired through a process of learning and practicing new habits and routines.

I am not claiming that you can instantly become a genius by applying certain techniques or by developing specific habits. But by making some basic changes discussed in this and other chapters, you can indeed see improvement in your overall mental abilities. I'm sure you can see how improving your mind's sharpness can benefit musical skill.

Some examples of musical situations that can benefit from a sharpened mind are: the study of music theory, substituting chord voicing's, figuring second or third harmony for backing vocals, or learning a song list after joining a new group. These are just a few examples of situations that musicians can find mentally challenging. Plain and simple - the sharper your mind is, the better off you'll be as a musician.

Scientific research has determined that intelligence is only 25% to 30% genetically inherited. Surprisingly, one's eye color and height are far more a result of heredity than intelligence. The human brain seems to be a naturally individualized "blank slate" and therefore has a natural capacity for improvement. This concept is the basis of what is discussed in this book. In the quest for improving one's musical skill, learning scales and practicing will only achieve limited results unless certain mental shortcomings are overcome (or at least minimized).

To summarize mental sharpness regarding biology - it is a combination of proteins, neurons, and receptors that make up the brain's neurotransmitter system. But enough of the science, for our purposes we just need to know the specific techniques that can be incorporated into our personal habits. These techniques will actually stimulate the chemical changes that will result in better mental performance (and thus better musical performance).

Humans have been designed with the ability to physically adapt to changing demands placed on the body. If a person moves from Florida to Maine in January, his or her nervous system will adapt to the cold. If one changes jobs from accounting to piano moving, his or her muscles will strengthen and grow to handle the physical demand of lifting heavy weight.

The brain also maintains a natural ability to adapt to new demands placed on it. It has been shown through neurological research that the speed of neural transmission can increase with repetition (this will be discussed more in the chapter on dexterity). Mental stimulation from added demands will change not only the brain's chemistry but also its actual physical structure. This can happen at any age but is more pronounced in youth. A dramatic example of brain growth is when a person's brain is damaged in an accident or stroke. It is common for people with damaged brains to regain mental function (to varying degrees) after performing extensive mental exercises.

Other examples are cases where artists have had left hemisphere damage, thus interfering with their ability to perceive spatial relations (judging sizes, distances, depth, etc.) This, of course, will prevent them from painting realistic portraits or landscapes. But after continuous mental exercise, many of these artists have regained the ability to judge distances and shapes. In this case, the right hemisphere of the brain has compensated for damage to the left hemisphere. Mental exercises can teach the brain how to reroute signals, thus finding alternate neurochemical pathways. It has also been found that a damaged brain will develop increased blood flow, resulting in higher levels of oxygen that can help compensate for impaired brain function.

Any mental activity will exercise the brain, but as with lifting weights if you don't do it consistently then you won't see any results. You have to reach a point of exertion before the growth process really kicks in. Reading is a good example. Most of us read at least a little every day, but if you were to read over an hour or two a day your brain would receive a very beneficial workout. Reading is one of the best things you can do for your brain. There's two ways to look at this - people read because they're smart, but they're also smart because they read. The store of knowledge that's gained through reading will help one's intelligence, but in reality, the main benefit of reading is the large amount of electrochemical activity that takes place during the act of reading. This electrochemical workout increases the brain's overall strength.

Puzzles and "brain teasers" are other exercises that can improve mental sharpness - whether it's the daily crossword puzzle, a cryptogram, or a similar puzzle, these mind games will exercise your brain's electrical and chemical functions. Most people think these activities are solely recreational but for our purposes here they are the brain's equivalent of lifting weights in a gym. Completed on a regular basis, puzzles can result in major mental improvements.

The next type of mental stimulation can be done with sound or light rhythms. We've discussed this several times already. It's been proven that light or sound pulses, generated by various devices and timed to certain rhythms, can stimulate the brain to follow the pulse of that rhythm.

To summarize, brain wave frequencies will affect the mind as follows:

Alpha state - 8 to 12 cycles per second - your everyday state of mind, not too relaxed, not too hyper
Beta state - 13 to 25 cycles per second - ranging from energetic to hyper, to panicked
Delta state - .5 to 3 cycles per second – sleep, a totally unconscious state.
Thera state - 4 to 7 cycles per second - very relaxed and tranquil.

Electroencephalogram (EEG) tests that have been performed while a subject is listening to certain pulses have shown that the brain can follow the rhythm that is set by these pulses. By slowing down the brain to the thera state, for example, a person can experience the benefits associated with that state – namely being open to deep levels of change and improvement. This is the basic reasoning behind the rhythmic chanting that monks and yogis use before meditation. The rhythm that is established by certain chants will slow down the brain's electrical tempo which helps bring on the thera state, thus leading to a deeper meditation.

The results of EEG's also suggest that certain parts of the brain begin to coordinate with each other when stimulated by certain pulses. The coordination that interests researchers is between the left and right hemispheres, the cerebellum and frontal lobes, and other regions of the brain that create a unified flow of mental energy that can improve mental performance.

There have been many tests conducted at various institutions on the effects of sound and light pulses on mental states. Some tests include the short-term measuring of brain activity and the testing of IQ. Others have measured concentration, dexterity, and other mental energies. Measurements have been taken before and after subjects have undergone sessions of specific sound and light rhythms, and the results are almost always positive. Other studies involved long-term observation of people who were given daily light and sound sessions. All these tests prove the same theory: the brain can be controlled through external rhythm, either directly or as part of other techniques.

But how can you put this information to use? There has been a whole market of consumer-grade electronic sound and light-pulsing devices that have sprung up as a result of this research. Probably the best book detailing the various devices, their specific applications, and the names and addresses of the manufacturers is "Mega Brain Power: Transform Your Life With Mind Machines and Brain Nutrients" by Michael Hutchison (Hyperion 1994). The Internet can also provide information about these types of devices, where to buy them, their cost, etc.

I would highly recommend that before you purchase such a device, first study the overall subject of brain waves and any information that is included with the device before attempting to make any radical changes to your brain's current rhythm. I'm not implying that there is anything wrong with slowing down your brain wave frequency before a meditation session (which is probably the most common use of such a device). However, I am advising that you learn about the overall subject before using these types of devices on a regular basis. If light and sound therapy is incorporated into a well-rounded program of mind improvement, meditation, mental exercise, and concentration development, you will be better able to maximize the benefits if you studied the science a little bit.

Another simple way to take advantage of sound pulse therapy is to buy one of the many audio cassettes on the market that contain specific audio pulses put to the background of classical music (or soft jazz, etc.). These cassettes can create a subliminal mental stimulation which relates to whichever pulse is being played. The specific frequency is usually listed with the title of each song so the listener can predict the resulting effect it will have on them. Certain songs will stimulate energy, and other songs will foster relaxation.

Music has also been proven to stimulate the release of endorphins as well as other chemicals. Studies have shown the positive effects of pain relief and increased alertness after listening to certain types of jazz, baroque, classical, and/or new world music. This is an interesting chain of events; listening to music can result in the sharpened mental abilities needed to improve your musical talents.

CDs, cassettes, and software have existed for years that are designed to develop specific abilities beneficial for musicians. The first type is designed to improve the mind's ability to process sound. With practice and testing, the brain can be trained to memorize pitches, intervals, and chords even without any reference point. This may seem amazing to many people - but if you can memorize the smell of a rose versus the smell of a wet dog, then it's also possible to memorize an A flat versus a D sharp.

In addition to these well-known pitch-training aids, another type of hearing improvement tool exists that will strengthen the ears muscles and improve overall hearing. The process involves many different modes, but the basic one is when the listener tunes into alternating pitches (low, high, low, high, etc.) for a sustained period. This forces the tiny muscles in the ear to expand and contract over and over, strengthening the muscles much like curling a dumb-bell strengthens the arm. Musicians who have used this method for long periods have claimed that the improved ability to hear also improves pitch recognition as well as other ways of processing sound.

Light also has major effects on your mental and physical well-being. It's well known that daylight triggers the body to produce chemicals needed for good health and mental clarity. In northern Alaska for example (where the earth's rotation about the sun creates a unique cycle of extended daylight and darkness), it is common for people to develop incredible boosts of energy and mental sharpness during the period of constant daylight. And of course just the opposite is true during the extended darkness; many people develop depression, physical ailments and intense mental malaise. Aside from these common occurrences in northern climates, researchers have conducted many other tests to prove the effects of light on people.

The effects of light on people's mental state have become so well known that special, non-fluorescent lights are commonly installed in offices and work areas to maximize workers effectiveness, mental sharpness, energy levels, and emotional well-being. It has even been known by insurance companies that long periods of exposure to poor lighting can lead to sickness and accidents due to mental haziness.

Along the same lines as sound and light pulsing is the simple effect of motion. As any high-strung person can tell you, the act of tapping one's foot or rocking back and forth is a necessary outlet for nervousness. But motion serves as more than a display of nervous energy; it is also the result and a reinforcement of the mind's wave patterns. One of the reasons that it's important to rock a baby back and forth in your arms is that it's been proven to stimulate the nervous system, activating the fluids of the inner ear, sending impulses to the cerebellum, and creating a flow of electrochemical energy through the brain and nervous system.

Research has shown that motion, either in the form of dancing or rocking back and forth, before a test or other mental challenge can improve your performance. One of the reasons for this is that motion creates a flow of nerve impulses through the brain in such a way that a better harmony between the left and right hemispheres is generated. As mentioned in regard to meditation, the better the coordination between the different regions of the brain (especially between the left and right hemispheres), the better the brain's overall functioning. You should also keep active when you are practicing your music, whether it's moving with the beat as you play or avoiding long periods of stillness when studying.

It's become standard practice for many people with desk jobs (or jobs that inherently have long periods of physical inactivity) to get up and walk, stretch, or use a gym if provided (many larger companies now have small gyms on their premises for this reason). This practice has helped with stress relief and improving overall health, but it has also become recognized that physical motion can improve mental performance.

Many of these mind control techniques came to the public's attention in the1980's, which has come to be known as the self-improvement (or "me") decade. The science of mind improvement gained large popularity around that time. The media began to focus on any new self improvement technique or discovery of newly defined mental disorders (such as A.D.D. – Attention Deficiet Disorder). One of the most popular of the newly publicized mind improvements was Biofeedback (although Biofeedback had been around for decades). Biofeedback clinics began to spring up all over the US and Europe. This treatment is performed by attaching sensors to the patient, monitoring blood pressure, pulse, breathing, and muscle tension. This allows the patient to actually visualize how tense or relaxed they are. The session then consists of exercises that promote relaxation or tension, allowing the person to see their body's reaction. This gives the person the ability to physically memorize the ability to relax, which many people cannot do naturally.

Similar to this are other types of bio-sensing devices, specifically EEG feedback. EEG (Electroencephalogram) feedback monitors the individual's brainwaves, giving results that determine how a certain mental activity stimulates certain parts of the brain. By using this type of biofeedback, you can make major improvements in mind power by making changes in your brain activity. This type of service can be located either online, in the phonebook, or through medical directories. It is a great way to monitor the success of your overall mind improvement techniques. For example, a before and after EEG can show improved coordination between brain regions after a meditation session. Or a series of visits can plot the improvement of brain activity over the course of weeks or months and allow you to see the benefits of the various mind-sharpening techniques found in this or other books. It can show you if you are on the right path or the areas in which you still need to improve. EEG feedback may seem a bit excessive of a tool in the quest for improving musical skill, but keep in mind that it is only an option for people who may be interested in taking mind power improvement to a higher level. Monitoring brain waves is only one way we can benefit from our knowledge of mental cycles.

Other than a steady rhythm of electrical pulses, our minds also follow longer-term cycles that range from 20 to 45 days. These are known as biorhythms. Many people are aware of the mind and body's cycle of high and low performance. Charts can be calculated, based on the day you were born, that will show you when you will be at your best or worst, based on different categories. The categories are intelligence, creativity, energy, sexuality, and physical stamina. There are also other categories being discovered all the time. For example, if you have your personal chart plotted you may see that

on May the 5th you will be at your best regarding intelligence and then for the next 33 days you will gradually
reduce in intelligence until the cycle hits the low point
on June 7th. Then over the next 33 days, your intelligence will gradually increase until it hits another high
point on July 10, etc. This doesn't mean that on June 7th
you will be a babbling idiot. You will always be within a
specific range. But on May 5th compared to June 7th
you will just see a moderate difference in your overall
intelligence.

Each category, such as creativity or energy, has a different number of days in it's cycle. Therefore, it is not always
easy to plot a complete chart of all these biorhythms.
However, there are many books that will show you how to
do as well as Web sites that will do it for you. To list just a
couple: biochart.com and arakni.com/biorhythm.

Some people will actually work their schedules around
these high and low points to optimize their performance
or to at least compensate for the differences. For example, if you are a runner and have a race scheduled on a day
that you will be at a relative low point in terms of physical
endurance, then you might want to get some extra sleep
the day before or take other steps to improve your stamina that you wouldn't otherwise take.

Not everyone believes that it's worth the effort to
measure their highs and lows, and that one should just
always do the best he/she can do, not worrying about
moderate differences in performance. But if as a musician
you are interested in your personal highs and lows, then
there are many ways to take advantage of this. Perhaps
you can keep your biorhythms in mind when you schedule

your gigs, plan sessions with a songwriting partner, or pre-pare for tests (if you are in school for music).

Other than long-term cycles that range from 20 to 45 days, the mind also works on a short-term rhythm that repeats approximately every hour. This cycle is easy to get the feeling for, especially if you are studying, composing, or practicing music. From the time you start, be aware of how focused and sharp you are. After about 45 to 60 minutes, you will notice a definite decline in concentration and clarity. At this point, it's usually good to take a break for about 5 minutes, or until you feel mentally rested. Then, begin your work again. After a while, you will see a pattern of mental highs and lows which will demonstrate your mind's own rhythm. You can then customize your work habits around this cycle.

In addition to optimizing performance, knowing your brain's rhythm can also be put to other uses. We discussed earlier how the brain has a wave frequency that varies from 4 to 25 cycles per second (while awake). Throughout the day, the brain will gradually fluctuate in frequency. These cycles of brain wave frequencies very closely coincide with the 45 to 60-minute cycle of mental performance that was mentioned before. During the approximate 5 to 10 minutes that you feel mentally slow (which is usually when you take a break), the mind is actually entering a semi-thera state and is operating at a slower frequency. Have you ever noticed that sometimes during the day you will get the "stares" and will feel very relaxed (or at least relatively relaxed)? This is when your mind enters the slower frequency stage. This is also a good time to medi-tate, because as we discussed before, the relaxed thera state is ideal for either meditation or self-hypnosis. After about 10 minutes in this state, the brain will then increase its wave frequency back up to between 8 to 12 cycles per second. This of course is an ideal time to get active again.

Aside from the types of mental exercises and brain rhythm awareness that have been mentioned thus far in this chapter, self-hypnosis (once again) is a very effective means to achieve improved brain function. Whereas the exercises will pinpoint specific skills, hypnosis will affect the subconscious – which exsists behind the skills. If brain exercises can be compared to lifting weights to improve muscle strength, then hypnosis is like nutrition that will improve the body's overall health.

Once again we have come across a subject that over-laps into other areas and chapters. Therefore, rather than discuss the process of self-hypnosis again, I'll refer you to the chapters on motivation and confidence. The only dif-ference is that instead of implanting subconscious habits of confidence, you can suggest improved mental habits, such as analyzing things deeper (constructing musical arrangements), applying logic to solving problems (as in figuring out chord substitutions), increasing your mental quickness (which is important for sight-reading), and other powers of the mind as they apply to writing, arranging, and performing music. What you would be doing here is creat-ing subconscious habits that may not actually strengthen the brain directly, just improve how you use the strengths you already have.

The self-hypnotic suggestions that can be used could be worded as follows: "I will focus my mind and concen-trate on things I am studying or the song I am playing";

"I will be patient and willing to spend time learning new information or songs"; "I can keep a steady beat and stay in time with any song I'm playing"; or "I have the discipline to practice my instrument for long hours".

Thus far this book has gone over the mind's capabilities on an intellectual level, but we all know there is much more to our minds than just intelligence. Emotions play a big part in our thinking and actions, and they too should be optimized to truly improve our abilities. Emotions are what truly make us human. It could take an entire chapter, or even book, to refer to all the research that has been done in this field. Many of the mental disorders that people suffer from are emotional in nature. It is a mental energy that can grow in strength until a person is overwhelmed, or mentally clouded. Have you ever had your heart broken and found yourself running red lights or forgetting to pay the electric bill? Despite any level of intelligence or logic, if your emotions begin to get the better of you, then you may as well be a total idiot. Despite any level of mind-power, your brain will not function properly.

When I began writing this book, I knew that I lacked any formal education in the field of psychology or neurology. What I intended to do was thoroughly research all of these different aspects of the mind and translate them in ways that could be applied by musicians to improve their abilities. The subject of emotional health, however, is a topic that is too intense, vague, and difficult to translate accurately. I've been very careful not to make personal interpretations of any of these findings other than how they can be used to sharpen the musical mind, although this specific subject may be the exception. Human emotional health is a science that has come a long way, but it is still very incomplete. The latest research seems to point to genetic traits or brain chemistry as being the most common reason for depression and other emotional problems.

There's no way we can deal with this level of self-improvement in this book. However, I can list a few common and safe ways that a person can begin to get a grip on their emotions. These methods have been around for a long time and are closely related to other mind control techniques. This may be an over-simplification of the situation, but if you think about the last time your emotions got the better of you, what were you doing a lot of? The answer ...thinking. Emotions can make you think, think and think some more. It's probably an instinctive way for us to try to overcome a problem - to think about it until we can correct the situation. Many times thinking can indeed be an effective way to figure out ways to deal with problems and to find solutions. For example - if you're writing a song and just can't seem to find the right lyrics, you may find yourself thinking for hours. But some people have a bad habit of thinking all the time, to the point of being more aware of their thoughts then what's going on around them (like driving down the road).

Thinking too much is an obvious problem that can interfere with concentration and other mental necessities. Meditation and other techniques found in the Concentration Chapter are effective ways to break this habit. In addition to these techniques, just an overall sense of being "here and now" will definitely sharpen your mind and improve your awareness. Emotional reasons are by far the leading cause of over-thinking. If you are sad about something, it will lead to excessive thinking and therefore, lead to a sluggish mental state that will dramatically interfere with your playing, memory, focus, and every other musical ability.

It would be inappropriate for me to suggest ways to overcome emotional turmoil (that leads to over thinking) other than the common approaches that have been used throughout the years. First, take action to resolve the problem that is causing the strong emotions. Simple to say, but usually difficult to do. For example, if your girlfriend or boyfriend has broken up with you, there are some cases where action can win him or her back. For example, if he or she is fed up with your gambling, then you just have to decide which is more important, your love- life or the fun of gambling. This is a no-brainer, but often people will overlook it. If your music is being interfered with by your lack of concentration, which is caused by excessive thinking, which is the result of overwhelming emotions, caused by your loved one leaving you, and finally, which is because of a gambling problem (just an example, of course), then you can correct the whole chain by using some self-discipline to quit gambling.

Second, if there's nothing that can be done to change the situation that is causing you grief (perhaps a loved one just passed away), then the only thing you can control is excessive thinking. Now, of course, a strong emotion will cause us to think about it, and in the case someone close dying, you will obviously be giving the sad situation some thought. But to think, and think, and think about something that is hurting you won't change reality at all. You have to make the conscious decision to think about it for only a certain amount of time, then clear your head and focus your mind on the outside world. This too is easier said than done but there are many techniques discussed in this book that will help to turn off that inner activity and focus on the real "here and now" world (meditation being the most effective one).

Third is involving yourself completely with an activity to help get your mind off of the emotion. Being a musician you have an obvious outlet. This can be a complete cycle - to overcome emotions that are clouding your mind and interfering with your musicianship; you can focus your mind on practicing music.

The last approach is one that many people use...spirituality. I'm not going to preach to you here, but many people feel a rock-solid fullness in their life from religion. It allows you to focus on an energy larger than yourself. This can be a whole subject in itself, but for our purpose here let's just summarize it by saying that when you apply your awareness to a higher level, such as God (however you want to define God), it can add a lot to your life. In the case of healing emotions and controlling excessive thought, the higher consciousness that religion can bring is a very widely accepted practice. To some religious people, it may sound selfish only to seek religion as a means to heal painful emotions, and there are definitely other reasons why you would want to seek out a higher consciousness, but that's another subject in itself.

To summarize our discussion of emotions, just be aware that intense emotional pain can cripple your musical ability (and if that happens, it certainly won't make you feel any better). The main reason for this is the preoccupation that emotions can cause, which is a major obstacle to focus and concentration. If you are experiencing emotional pain, deal with it in positive ways that will allow you to keep your mind sharp and focused, which is a necessity for musical skill.

The last topic that we'll deal with in this chapter is diet. In the chapter on memory improvement, we discussed diet and how certain foods and supplements can sharpen the memory. But on a larger level, diet and supplements can also do wonders for the mind's overall strength and sharpness. I truly hope that you don't skip over this section because it sounds boring or like too much trouble. This may be one of the most important sections of the entire book. Nothing affects your playing more than your brain and nervous system, and nothing affects your brain and nervous system more than the chemicals you put into your body.

When I was younger, it always bored me hearing someone preach about healthy diet, balanced meals, and nutrition. I didn't bother to eat healthy foods, and I still felt fine. But as I entered my thirties I started to feel some aches and pains, stiffness in the morning, gradually declining energy, and other telltale signs of a body that had been operating for over 10, 000 days. Having always been interested in cars and being mechanically inclined, I began to realize that the body is a machine, and I started to think of it in mechanical terms. Once I saw this new perspective, I began better habits of exercise and nutrition. After several years of new health habits, I can honestly say that I feel better now at age 52 then I did when I was twenty. But more importantly for this book's purposes is how your health directly affects your mind and therefore your music.

It is impossible to ignore how nutrition and health affect the mind's sharpness, reflexes, memory, and imagination. The proteins and chemistry required for strong neurotransmitters are just one example of how musical skill is very dependent on nutrition and health. Have you ever had a bad cold and tried to play your instrument? Your playing wasn't good - admit it. But having a cold isn't really the best example. With a cold, a healthy person still has a strong enough nervous system and reserve of energy to compensate for the illness and play at least decently. But if you've been eating junk foods for years, getting no exercise, and doing other things that you know is bad for your health (smoking cigarettes, excessive alcohol, etc.), then the transmission of nerve signals from the brain to the fingers, the recalling of information stored in the brain, and other electrochemical activity can actually be reduced far more than compared to just having a cold.

This is truly important stuff to know. It's absolutely critical for mental strength and good musicianship. I'm not insisting that you follow all the rules of nutrition and good health. I realize that a lot of people smoke cigarettes (I used to), and also eating well is difficult when you're on the road and only have time for fast food. But even if you just make a moderate attempt to limit the bad things and increase the good things, it's better than doing nothing. I would suggest exploring the subject of good health through books, the Internet, or even visiting a doctor or nutritionist. Rather than go into detail here, I'm just going to list some basic points that can be followed to sharpen the mind through nutrition.

Limit: nicotine, caffeine, sodium, fats, sugar, alcohol, fast foods or foods with chemical additives, prescription drugs that cause drowsiness, and foods high in cholesterol. These items, aside from having overall negative effects on your health, interfere specifically with brain and nervous system functions, and therefore affect your playing. As far as the prescription drugs, always tell your doctor that you are a serious musician and need to be mentally sharp and quick. Perhaps he can think of medicine that doesn't cause drowsiness and sluggishness, or at least reduce the amount of times per day that he wants you to take the drug.

Include (on a daily basis): a multi-vitamin, extra vitamin C / E / and B complex, certain amounts of protein, amino acids, calcium, magnesium, lecithin, beta carotene, phosphorus, potassium, iron, manganese, selenium, iodine, focalin, biotin, fruits, fish, vegetables, and at least 8 glasses of water. This list should be in addition to a balanced diet, and the vitamins and minerals, such as B complex and iron, should be taken as directed. Vitamins and minerals only work when taken in correct proportions. If you take, for example, 5 times the directed amount of potassium, then it's not going to be five times as good for you. It may even have some serious side effects. The key here is balance.

If you really want to achieve a high level of mental sharpness, then in addition to developing a good diet, there are many supplements that have been developed over the years to strengthen the brain and nervous system's chemical functioning. With the support of a nutritionist, some of these "smart drugs" can be prescribed (some don't need a prescription), and when used in conjunction with a good diet, amazing mental clarity and performance can be achieved.

The following is a list of some of the most common "smart drugs": RNA(ribonucleic acid), Isoprinosine, vasopressin, Hydergine, Prl-8-53, L-prolyl/l-leucyl/glycine amide(a compound), Deaner, choline, magnesium pemoline, Ritalin, Nootropyl, and ACTH 4-10. Although these drugs are an option, there's really no need to go to all the trouble of using smart drugs when just a solid diet and controlling personal habits, such as smoking and junk food, will result in a sharper mind.

If you really want to do it right, go to a nutritionist (it shouldn't cost more than $100), tell them that you want to achieve mental sharpness and quick reflexes for playing music, and they can customize a diet and supplement routine based on your weight, age, lifestyle, and overall health. They may even want to do some blood analysis to see if you have any deficiencies or incorrect levels of enzymes. Then a tailored plan can be designed to fully optimize your health and mental powers.

For those of you who feel that they are already mentally sharp despite unhealthy lifestyle and poor diet, you may simply just be used to how you feel mentally and have adapted to it. But if you were to make the necessary changes to your health habits and kept track of how you performed mentally, you will be surprised at how the mind really does improve. This will of course directly affect your music in numerous ways. I have listed many different techniques and plans for sharpening the mind, and just the information in this chapter alone will have dramatic effect on your playing.

In conclusion, a person who is clumsy and dim-witted will not be able to become a serious musician. The intense coordination, reflexes, thought processes, memory, and focus required to achieve a high level of playing makes it a necessity to first work on your mental abilities. The amount of time involved in using these various techniques is not that much at all. But even if it was, it'll be well worth the effort. Perhaps just doing one mind-sharpening technique per day, then practicing your instrument, as usual, will be sufficient. There's no rush here. Just develop a habit of performing these mind improvement methods then go about your everyday business and forget about it. Then every few weeks analyze your abilities to see how you're coming along. Before you know it, you will have developed a sharper "musical mind."

9
Dexterity

DEXTERITY AND COORDINATION may seem like physical rather than mental issues, but without the mental functions of the brain, there can be no physical movement. Unlike lifting weights and eventually seeing a physical result, practicing a musical instrument leads to the development of brain signals through the nervous system. Thus, the aspect of hand-eye coordination and dexterity certainly does belong in this book. And by the way, singers also require dexterity for coordination of the diaphragm, lungs, larynx, and mouth.

There are many mental techniques for improving dexterity. A lot of them have already been discussed in other chapters, but regarding different aspects of musicianship. For example, concentration has been discussed as it relates to overall performance, learning, and even composition. But for the purpose of improving dexterity, it definitely needs to be expanded on again.

First, let's look at the process that takes place in the brain and nervous system when the fingers are moved in a pre-arranged sequence, such as when you're playing a simple melody on piano. The first thing that happens is that you make a conscious decision to move your finger. The signal is then relayed through the nerves until it reaches the finger and the muscles move. What happens next is that another signal is sent back to the brain with feedback that tells it what just happened and if it was successful. A loop is created by the command sent to the fingers, and the feedback sent back to the brain.

If the melody is slow enough, you can consciously become aware of the movement before the next note is played. But if you are playing a very fast series of notes, then you may not be aware of the feedback until after a few notes are finished being played. You become aware of clusters of notes and not the individual notes. This is because the brain can either send commands or receive feedback, but it can't do both at the same time. Have you ever noticed that if you're playing a slow piece of music, you may be reaching for a certain note, then at the last second you may realize that you are about to hit the wrong note and you correct yourself? This is because there's time to receive feedback and analyze that feedback with the memory of what note needs to be played. You can then adjust the finger's movement and shift towards the correct note. But when you are playing a rapid-fire series of notes, only after a certain amount of notes are finished are you aware of any mistakes and can make adjustments if the sequence needs to be done again. And even when you do analyze your playing and make last second corrections, the interruption to your conscious flow can sometimes cause you to stumble and lose the beat, or may even interfere with your memory of what's coming next.

The point of all this is that for music to be performed accurately and fast if need be, then it's hard to do it *and* consciously analyze your brain's feedback at the same time. Therefore, the physical aspects of performance are done at a subconscious level, and your consciousness is only aware of the *overall* sounds, tempo, arrangement, interplay with other musicians, and other aspects of the big picture.

To further expand on how to streamline the flow of electrochemical signals through the nervous system, let's look at just how complex this path is. The signal that starts in the brain and continues to the fingers must pass through and interact with the following regions: cerebral cortex, cerebellum, pontie nuclei, cerellar penduncle, cerebellar nuclei, frontal lobe, thamamus, corticospinal tract, ventrolateral nucleus, and of course, the spinal cord itself. As described before, this path is used for both sending the initial signal as well as receiving feedback from the muscles regarding the execution of the action. Also, this path is not simply a straight line but requires constant interaction and coordination between the various parts.

With such a complex series of actions and reactions, it's amazing that the fingers are able to receive any signals at all. But add to this the conscious awareness of the process, and the signal then needs even more complex interactions. This is what happens when you over-think what you are doing. Not only does the signal have to return to the brain with feedback, but now it has to sidetrack to the cerebral hemispheres to consciously analyze the whole process, which also requires many other changes to the signal path. To summarize this, you are making a difficult job even more complex when you consciously think about your movements, making it almost impossible for the fingers to accurately perform musically.

To further expand on the argument of limiting your thinking during playing, let's look at some examples of sports psychology. It's been known for years that great athletes who are on a hot streak will say that they really don't even think about what they're doing, they just do it. To test this notion, experiments have been done where golfers wore electrodes placed on their heads measuring brain activity. About ten different golfers participated in the experiment, which lasted a few days. The golfers practiced putting and were tested to see how many straight putts they could make. After the experiment, the EEG measurements of their brain activity showed that the best golfers had very little brain activity, especially in the left hemisphere, which indicated that they weren't thinking or analyzing their movements.

All of this shows one very important fact - there's a big difference between focusing on what you're doing and thinking about what you're doing. To improve your playing as a musician, you must learn how to stop over-analyzing your movements. To reduce conscious control of your playing, you must replace it with subconscious control. Many musicians refer to this as "finger memory". Have you ever been playing your instrument when someone asks you a question or begins a conversation? Many times you just continue playing while you carry on the conversation. It's as if there's two of you, one talking and one playing the instrument. This is finger memory (although it doesn't always have anything to do with "conscious" memory).

You can also be improvising, just playing random riffs, and carry on a conversation. I guess that could be called "finger improvisation." Either way, the fingers aren't the ones doing all this work, but rather it's the subconscious mind. This is the ability you must work at in order to become a truly great player. Once you have a song perfectly memorized, your playing should be done with auto-pilot (your subconscious) while your consciousness only watches the big picture. Examples are: following the arrangement of the song, receiving feedback from other musicians and staying in the rhythm along with them, keeping aware of the songs overall flow, etc.

Let's look at another example of over-thinking. Have you ever watched the second hand on a clock and consciously became very aware of it as it moves from second to second? Over the course of time, its movement will become distorted and will seem to be speeding up and slowing down. Tempo is a common trouble area for many musicians and staying in beat is sometimes more difficult than it seems. Even with a natural sense of rhythm, a musician will fade in and out of tempo if they are becoming too aware of it. The more over-focused they become on the beat, the more they will actually falter. But if they remove the conscious control of their timing and just relax and let the auto-pilot (subconscious) take over, they will notice a definite improvement.

Only as a beginner, or during the learning process of a certain song or solo, does conscious awareness of your movements have a place. Once you consciously analyze your playing of a song (i.e. with guitar, the position, scale, key, etc.; with drums, the sequence of snare / bass / hi-hat hits, etc.), you then proceed to the next step which is placing all that information into the subconscious. This is done with practice and constant repetition. It is said that a great musician is just another member of the audience when it comes to sitting back and watching their fingers move and hearing what is being played. This is because on a conscious level, someone else *is* playing - their subconscious.

This isn't that amazing when you think about it. When was the last time you consciously performed all the movements required to walk? Probably when you were two. Once you mastered the act of walking, the movements were all placed into subconscious control, and you no longer had to be aware of them. Now you can look around, carry on a conversation or even read a magazine as you walk, just as if someone was carrying you on their back. Your legs don't need your conscious control; they're under the control of autopilot. With this in mind, there are many things that can be done to improve the brain's ability to play music with the subconscious auto-pilot. For the most part, good old-fashioned practice, and lots of it is still the way to do this. However, as with recent advancements in sports psychology, there are many new techniques for sharpening the mental processes needed to perform at your best.

Let's first look at a very interesting discovery that researchers have uncovered regarding the subconscious mind and physical activity. An experiment was performed at a university designed to evaluate the strength of the subconscious versus the conscious mind as they pertain to dexterity. Three groups of students were formed, about

50 to a group, and the one thing all the students had in common was that they had never played basketball. The first group then spent several weeks practicing shooting baskets. The second group was allowed to practice shooting baskets for awhile, then sat in comfortable chairs, closed their eyes, and visualized shooting baskets. The third group also was allowed to shoot baskets for awhile, but they then were told not to play or visualize shooting baskets at all.

At the start of the experiment, the groups were tested to see how many baskets they could make. Then after the two weeks they were retested to see how their score had improved or changed. Group three, who didn't practice or visualize, showed no improvement (of course), group one (who were allowed to actually practice on the court) showed an 80% improvement and group two (who used their minds to visualize shooting baskets) showed a 50% improvement. These results showed the actual power of the subconscious mind regarding re-creating physical movement. Although group #2 didn't improve as much as group #1, they were close enough to demonstrate how important the mind is regarding physical activity. When an activity is visualized carefully enough to simulate reality, the subconscious cannot tell the difference. When group #2 visualized shooting baskets, they carefully imagined the feel and weight of the ball, the amount of force needed to shot the ball far enough to hit the basket, and every other feel and sense they experienced when they actually practiced. It re-created the movements and necessary coordination almost as if they were really performing the action.

We've all awakened from a bad dream with our heart racing. Or if you're dreaming about suffocating or drowning, you will wake up gasping for air. This shows how the subconscious sends signals to the body as if the dream was really happening. The fact that the subconscious can't tell reality from imagined situation is the basis of much of what's detailed in this book. And many of the breakthroughs in sports psychology are also based on this.

How can this knowledge be of any use? It's not suggested that you replace actual practice with imagined practice, but the visualization of playing a difficult piece or even just running through scales should be *added* to your basic practice routine. The subconscious mind may be capable of amazing things, but overall it is very stupid and is easily tricked. Just as we learned how to trick it into developing confidence with regard to overcoming stage fright, it can also be tricked into achieving incredible finger dexterity.

Aside from your usual everyday practice (which can never be replaced) make it a point to sit down and perform a short self-hypnosis session after each practice. Or when standing in line at the bank, for example, you can practice scales or drum rudiments with your mind. Go through all the steps that were detailed in previous chapters for creating a self-hypnotic state, then imagine your fingers moving with incredible speed and accuracy (or your voice projecting with strength and accuracy). Imagine the most amazing performance conceivable. Be sure to use all the techniques for effective visualization. Visualize seeing the sights, hearing the sounds, the feeling of the instrument, the room temperature, as well as any smells that would be in the room (incense, the dog sitting nearby, etc.). As long as you make the scene as lifelike as possible and use the relaxation techniques for achieving the correct brain waves, the subconscious will actually believe that it is really happening and will over time implant the capability into its storage.

This method only works if your actual skill level is at least reasonably advanced enough to make the jump. If an absolute beginner with limited dexterity were to try this, they might see some improvement, but this technique only builds on what's already there. It can't create something from nothing. After many hours of real practice, the various regions of the brain and nervous system achieve a strong neurological adjustment to the rapid flow of signals to the fingers. Then by imagining an improvement to this condition, you are just increasing what has already been established. An unskilled player hasn't developed this neurological state enough for the subconscious to have anything to work with.

As long as we're on the subject of self-hypnosis, let's review some other ways it can be used to accelerate our playing, in this case, a live performance. One sure-fire way to get ready for a gig is to prepare your mind and body before the show by using self-hypnosis. The usual routine for preparing for a gig is to warm up (using scales and exercises) and possibly a band rehearsal. Then once at the club you must endure the seemingly endless wait to get up on stage, during which time you are trying to keep calm and mentally prepare for the show. This is the perfect time to find a quiet place and perform an intense self-hypnosis session. I always found my car, parked in a secluded corner of the parking lot, to be a good place. Or if you live nearby you can perform a session at home. However, it's best to come out of the hypnosis session as soon before the actual performance as possible. A self-hypnosis session won't be as effective if you live two hours away and have to deal with traffic.

In the chapter on confidence, where we dealt with overcoming stage fright, it was recommended to use self-hypnosis before a show to reinforce confidence and focus. In addition to those aspects of the performance, you now can add a pre-established mental routine to maximize your dexterity whereby you imagine yourself playing your instrument (or singing) with great ability and precision. Using your memory to recall times in the past when you were at your best, and using your imagination to see yourself pushing past that level of skill, you can envision (and feel) yourself playing a perfect performance. Self-hypnosis for building confidence and for preparing dexterity will both have a lot in common and will use images of you playing your best to achieve the same objective. After all, confidence and dexterity are inter-related to begin with, as discussed earlier. As I've also mentioned, self-hypnosis takes practice, and considering how valuable it is for so many aspects of music; you should carefully read all of the instructions I've included in this book and also study the subject yourself. Tutorials found on the Internet should do although a class or personal instructor would be even better.

As mentioned before, other chapters in this book will also have a definite effect on your dexterity. It would be wise to re-read certain chapters, but with a specific

perspective of applying the information directly to improving dexterity. Those chapters are:

Concentration - although it may seem to contradict
what we just discussed regarding not focusing too deeply
on the specific mechanical movements involved in playing,
you still must have your mind focused on the music and
not drifting off. A solid concentration will prevent distractions from interrupting the attention needed to maintain
a rhythm, follow the arrangement, shift positions, change
scales and chords, etc.

Mental sharpness - overall mental clarity and sharpness are definitely needed for strong dexterity. Music is
almost entirely a mental challenge, and the sharper you
are mentally, the better you will be as a musician.

Confidence- Positive thinking affects dexterity in
two ways. First, when performing in public, a lack of confidence makes a musician self-conscious. This not only
interferes with concentration but in an attempt to overcome that distraction, a musician then over-thinks his
movements. And as detailed before, this over-thinking
leads to a traffic jam in the brain. Secondly, confidence
has been proven time and time again, especially in sports
psychology, to allow the nervous system to operate at
its optimal efficiency. There's a number of theories why
this is so, many having to do with specific details of brain
function. But all that matters is that you are aware of
this fact and apply it to your playing and improving your
dexterity.

Memory - This doesn't directly affect your hand-eye
coordination, but the better you remember something,
the more accurate and faster you can perform it. Playing

a piece that you are struggling with to remember only interferes with the flow of nerve signals to the fingers. You may think that you have a song firmly memorized, but still may be consciously thinking of each part as you play it just to be sure. As mentioned before, this is a form of over-thinking that jumbles up the complex flow of signals through the nervous system that only leads to less than an optimal performance. When something is truly memorized, you should be able to play it perfectly while watching TV or carrying on a conversation. It will be placed into "auto-pilot", and the only thing your conscious mind has to do is sit back and watch or keep track of the big picture - like keeping the rhythm or adding some improvisational fill-ins or extra emotional coloring.

Another tool that has been used in previous chapters is meditation. Meditation has been proven to improve the coordination between the various parts of the brain, especially between the left and right hemispheres. Remember, the left hemisphere is mainly in control of technical and analytical activities, and the right side controls the expressive and artistic aspect of things. The coordination of the two is very important for musical dexterity. Although fast and accurate movement may seem to be more technical in nature, dexterity without expression and emotion will sound very mechanical and cold.

Relaxation is also very important for dexterity. This may be a physical aspect of playing. However it first requires a mental state before the physical condition can be achieved. It's been proven that tense muscles aren't capable of optimum movement and accuracy. There are a few reasons for this.

First - for a muscle to move, it first must relax or un-tense. This happens so quickly that you don't even notice it. When a signal gets to the muscle telling it to contract, the muscle first releases all tension and goes limp, then begins the movement. If the muscle is already relaxed, it takes much less time to prepare for the contraction and the movement can begin much quicker. By relaxing your muscles, you are putting them in "ready mode" thus sav-ing time and energy. With an intricate series of move-ments, such as playing a melody on trumpet, there are a lot of contractions that must be made. When you play with relaxed hands, you save unnecessary unclenching of the finger muscles every time they need to contract.

This is simple mechanical efficiency. You may think that this is more of a physical technique, and of course, this book is about mental aspects of musicianship. However if tensing up is a habit, then mental intervention is needed to break the habit. The phenomenon of most habits is that they go unnoticed, mainly because they are subcon-scious as opposed to conscious actions. So the first step of removing a habit is to first become very conscious of it. A common technique of making a conscious note of tension is to tense, then relax, tense, then relax, etc. This allows you to compare the two feelings and become more aware of how tension feels so that you can spot it easily.

This technique can be applied to playing a musical instrument by first playing something with tensed mus-cles, then playing the same thing with relaxed muscles, then back and forth. This exercise will magnify the feeling of tension and enable you to make the change from tensed playing to relaxed playing. Some people may be confused about the need for tension, especially if they play "tense music". If you play very fast and furious heavy metal guitar or drums, for example, it is still important to relax the muscles. This doesn't mean that when it's time to make a movement that the result will be relaxed and soft. You can still beat the hell out of your drums, and probably even better if you develop the habit of unclenching the muscles until it's time for action. Relaxing your playing merely refers to the neurological process of efficient mechanical movement.

The second reason is that relaxed playing is merely another way to un-clutter the already busy brain and nervous system so that the signals traveling from the brain to the muscles have a clear path. When the body is tensed, the subconscious interprets it as a conscious reaction to danger and responds by taking partial control of the nervous system. In times of actual danger, this allows the brain to send signals to the heart and adrenal glands (among many other parts of the body) which puts the body on guard and ready to fight or flee. The result is a lot of traffic traveling through the nervous system and the signals being sent to the fingers to play music is not considered to be a top priority in times of danger. Therefore, your ability to play is greatly reduced.

Another way to mentally improve dexterity is to become aware of "subconscious limiting". You may be subconsciously telling yourself that you lack talent and can only play at a certain level, or that you are a very good player but fear appearing cocky, egotistical, and/or flashy if you play full out. You may not be aware that this second condition even exists, but with some very conservative, mild-mannered people, the fear of appearing bold and too assertive will limit their playing. These people also try not to speak too loudly or dress too provocatively and overall are very unassertive. Any type of subconscious limiting of your musical abilities should be corrected, and the most direct and effective way to accomplish that is through self-hypnotism.

Another type of subconscious limiting is slowing down in order to play it safe. This is when you hold back your full out performance so that you can catch any mistakes. Mickey Mantle was one of the greatest home run hitters in the history of baseball, but he also struck out far more than average. If statistics were analyzed, most above-average home run hitters also strike out a lot. One reason for this is that they swing harder and give their hitting more effort, which results in two things. First, when they do make contact with the ball, it is hit very hard, resulting in many home runs. Second, because they swing harder, they aren't playing it safe, and the chances of missing the ball are increased. They consider this trade-off worthwhile by looking at the big picture.

A comparison can be made to music, although before coming to any conclusions let me explain. When you play it safe and play easily and slowly, sure you may make fewer mistakes, but by letting loose, you can let your playing push its limits and gradually improve. Only by pushing your limits can you ever pass those limits. The drawback of this may be that you will make more mistakes than if you just played it safe. However, unlike baseball, a musical mistake can be hidden, covered up, or even incorporated into the music. There are many ways to disguise mistakes.

When hitting a wrong note, just quickly raise it to a higher note (which is likely to fit somewhere in the scale) and it will sound as if you meant to do it. It's called a passing tone and is very common, especially in Blues and Rock. Or sloppy chords can be quickly changed to a staccato and you can focus on the root, thus reducing the effect of any bad notes. Even singers and drummers have tricks up their sleeves. There are many techniques for hiding mistakes, but then this only matters if you are performing for an audience. Otherwise, who cares if you mess up? You know that you are pushing your limits so that you can improve, so it shouldn't bother you. Gradually those mistakes will stop and you'll be at the next level of playing. Looking back, it will have been worth pushing your ability to the edge and allowing some bad notes, knowing that the result was a higher degree of playing.

Physical condition, health, and nutrition may not fall under the realm of the mind, although you can think of them as mental habits. Music may not involve as much physical stamina and exertion as sports (except maybe drumming), but it definitely requires a top-notch and healthy nervous system. Quick reactions and intense hand-eye coordination need to be maintained with good health. In the chapters on memory and mental sharpness, we discuss nutritional guidelines and additives for sharpening the mind. A balanced diet, basic vitamin and mineral supplements, regular exercise, and controlling or ending obvious health hazards (like smoking, excess alcohol, caffeine, etc.) is definitely beneficial for optimal physical coordination.

If super-charging your dexterity through specific nutritional routines and/or pharmaceutical supplements is something you'd be interested in, then a little research and experimenting may reveal some possibilities. It's well-known that everyone's metabolism is unique and you may find a specific diet that turns your fingers into blazing digits of steel.

And as long as we're discussing a few physical aspects of improvement, here's a little technique I came across that will also benefit your dexterity. The human nervous system is designed to favor one side or the other in terms of dexterity. We are either right-handed or left-handed. Most musical instruments require the use of both hands, however, and the improvement of overall dexterity will benefit from strengthening the ability of the weaker hand. One way to do this is to make it a habit to use the weak hand more often in everyday activities, such as opening doors, turning pages, pushing buttons, turning knobs, holding a fork, or even writing. This will require a new mental perspective, one which makes you think of movements and activities in a balanced way, not favoring one hand over the other. Throughout the course of the day, there's probably hundreds of movements that can be shifted to the other hand. Over time, this new habit will add dexterity to the weaker hand, and you may find that it will improve your playing.

Applying the techniques found in this chapter will indeed improve dexterity, but it still comes down to basic practice. Nothing mentioned here should be thought of as a shortcut, but rather a way to maximize or improve on the results of intense practice. The chapter on motivation will also improve dexterity by developing the desire to practice a lot. Certain mental habits such as not over-thinking will improve dexterity, but improving something and building something to begin with are two different things.

In conclusion; build dexterity first through intense practice, then fine-tune and sharpen your dexterity with the mental techniques found in this chapter. Now let's review some mental habits and techniques to optimize physical practice. These tips can help stimulate the electrochemical process that leads to improved dexterity. Scientific research has proven that the mind can affect the outcome of exercise and practice, so why not get the most from each hour of work.

We've all heard the expression "be the ball" in regard to coaches training their athletes. In golf, for example, it's a commonly known mental habit to put your awareness as the ball being hit and not as you hitting the ball. This different perspective has been proven to increase the accuracy of how the ball is hit and how hard. If the imagination is used strongly enough the athletes perception of spatial relationships changes and the nervous system has a better feel or sense of the ball's distance, angle, etc. As "cosmic" and spacey as this may sound, it has been responsible for amazing results in athletic performance.

To apply this principle to musical practice, simply imagine that your body doesn't stop at your fingers, but continues into the instrument. Imagine that the instrument would bleed if stabbed or that you would feel it if someone were to hit it. Allow this change in perception to sink in, using self-hypnosis, creative visualization, and any other method for achieving this new mental image. It will probably take practice, so incorporate the new view into your routine of daily practice. Not only practice the new perception but use the new perception in your usual exercises, drills, scales, etc. This new spatial sense and adjustment to the nervous system's perception of motion and distance (with regard to your instrument) will have a major effect on your dexterity.

Even more important than all these techniques for optimizing practice is to do the practice to begin with. The only way to rack up thousands of hours of practice is to motivate yourself into wanting to practice. It is possible to still practice a lot even though your interest and desire are lacking, but it's rare, difficult and will even reduce how much you get out of the practice. We already discussed this in the chapter on motivation, and the various techniques should be re-read and applied here.

In conclusion: if practicing your instrument was the most fun you could imagine having, then you wouldn't even have to try to improve, it would just happen and big time. So if you can trick your mind into feeling that practice is incredible fun, this alone could turn you into a master musician. All the other techniques would still be useful methods for improvement (enhancing creativity, overcoming stage fright, etc.), but as far as dexterity, you would be on auto-pilot headed towards an intense level of skill. It would just be a matter of time.

Have fun while practicing. If practice seems like a dreadful and boring activity, it will be very hard to continue a steady schedule day after day. It may even turn you off music altogether. This is a job for self-hypnosis (what else?). As we mentioned before, if you can motivate yourself using self-hypnosis that practice is the most fun you could have, then you would find it hard not to practice. The rest all falls into place.

The best way to get the most out of practice is to focus. That means turning off the TV and shutting the door. However motivated we may be, we still want to live an enjoyable life. Let's face it - TV and the Internet are a big part of most people's lives. Any motivated musician will practice as much as possible every day, and by practice I mean turning off the TV, logging off the Internet, and focusing specifically on your exercises, drills, and practice routine. But *in addition* to focused practice, you can benefit from practicing while watching TV, as long as you're probably going to watch a little TV anyway. The easiest example of this is with an unplugged electric guitar, sitting on the couch, and playing scales while watching the tube. If you figure all the hours every year that you watch TV, it would surely add up if you could kill two birds with one stone and do scale exercises or drum rudiments (with a rubber pad) while watching your favorite shows.

Aside from guitar and drums, other instruments can also be practiced on the couch. Piano players can have a small Casio type keyboard on their laps and play it with the volume set low. Sax and horn player scan practice their fingering without necessarily blowing. And there's even techniques that singers can use to work on breath and diaphragm control without actually singing out loud. Once again, this is meant to be an addition to practice, not a replacement. If you are practicing a focused session and the thought of TV comes to mind, don't feel that you can finish your practice with the above method of playing while watching TV. I will be causing you a great disservice if I implant this thought into your mind. Never replace even a minute of focused practice for "TV practice". If you are serious about your music, then only after the regular amount of focused practice, you can add a little extra practice in by playing while watching TV.

Be warned, TV and the Internet have interfered with many a musician developing great talent. It's a temptation that can prevent you from ever achieving a great level of skill. If you are truly dedicated and focused, you'd probably get rid of your TV altogether (computers, however, can be a great benefit with all the great sites for musicians). But realistically, as long as you follow my above advice and are disciplined about it, you can still become a great player and watch occasional TV or surf the Internet.

In the above section, I mention *focused* practice. It's one thing to turn the TV off, go into a separate room and close the door. But aside from removing all external distractions, many of us still have problems with concentrating. By re-reading the chapter on concentration and applying it to practice, you will be able to get much more out of each hour of practice. When you fully focus during practice, the nervous system and brain are absorbing the actions, movements, memory and feeling at a much deeper level. It can be shown how one hour of focused practice can achieve the same results as 3 or 4 hours of unfocused practice. It makes no sense to spend the time and get much less out of each hour then you potentially could.

Here's a neat trick - practice with your eyes closed now and then. This is somewhat related to item #1 above, where I mention to "be the instrument." By developing such oneness with your instrument, you can actually feel where the notes are, definitely creating a strong level of dexterity. One of the reasons police ask suspected drunk drivers to stand straight, close their eyes, and touch the tips of their nose with their fingertip is to test their overall level of equilibrium, balance, and dexterity. If they were allowed to keep their eyes open, it would be allot easier. Without sight, the brain doesn't have the point of reference it is used to relying on and has to struggle to perceive distance and size. If you can increase your nervous system's ability to feel distance, space, and proportion, it will also improve its functions of movement, hand position, finger placement, etc. If you practice "blind playing", it will definitely strengthen your overall dexterity. Perhaps just 5 to 10 minutes per practice session would be sufficient. This may not be a mental aspect of playing, but it's something I uncovered in my research that is based on the functioning of the brain and nervous system.

Try this experiment: for a few days in a row meditate for at least 20 minutes before practicing. Try to put yourself into the most relaxed state of mind and body you can imagine, then start your usual practice routine. After about a week go back to not meditating before practice. Now compare the difference. Did you feel more focused, more dexterous, more musical when meditating first? It's been pointed out several times in this book how meditation affects the entire nervous system and brain, but it was usually in regard to mental aspects of playing; concentration, imagination, and confidence. But meditation has a very strong effect on the brain and nervous system's balance, flow of nervous impulses, reaction, and movement. Don't make the mistake of thinking that the relaxed state created by meditation will slow you down if you play a quick-paced type of music. As previously mentioned, it's a definite fact that relaxed muscles are more responsive to signals from the brain and will move quicker and with more precision.

We previously stressed the importance of not over-thinking movements and physical actions when playing, but rather to let the subconscious deal with a majority of the work. This frees up the conscious mind for focusing on the musical flow, arrangement, and overall big picture. The only exception to this particular rule is to occasionally analyze your physical technique and motions while practicing. You don't want to make this a habit, so it would be wise to remind yourself that you are focusing on your hands and finger movements just for the purpose of implanting the memory of correct movement into your subconscious.

For example, you may be working on a song that requires rapid and drastic position shifts on guitar. It would be necessary to analyze and decide on the best way to arrange your fingering to quickly shift and grab a new chord. A few trail and errors may be needed until you find the most effective fingering. Then to memorize the finger positions, you would repeat the part over and over, while consciously concentrating on exactly how the fingers are positioned, the feeling of the shift and even the visual appearance of the chord fingering. Once you feel that you are comfortable with the part, you must then try not to think about it and just do it. It has now been implanted into your mind's auto-pilot, and your conscious mind can deal with the overall groove, arrangement, and coordination with the other players in the band.

As I've mention repeatedly, the different chapters of this book are inter-related with regard to how a certain technique can apply to different aspects of your musical skill and improvement. We've discussed the use of biorhythms previously and how they can be used to chart your nervous system's natural flow of strength and weakness. I've never suggested that you actually postpone or cancel a gig, but rather use your understanding of biorhythms to perhaps compensate for your lows. An example would be to rehearse exceptionally hard on the morning of a gig when your biorhythm indicates a low level of dexterity, concentration, confidence, or other important mental element. Biorhythms probably aren't as critical with regard to your practice sessions, but the awareness of your biorhythms can still be useful. The best case would be just the opposite of the previous example in which you compensate for low dexterity with extra rehearsal. For the purpose of practice, it would actually be beneficial to increase your practice during *high* levels of dexterity. The reason for this is that during your nervous system's optimal state, your brain's electrochemical flow, feedback from muscles, and coordination between the left and right hemispheres (as well as other regions of the brain) is running at its best. It would be an ideal time to have the subconscious memorize this state and how this mental and physical balance relates to your playing. You'll get far more out of practicing on days that you feel very dexterous as opposed to days that you feel clumsy. For this reason, plan very long practice sessions on days when your dexterity biorhythm is high. However, don't use a low biorhythm as an excuse for reducing practice.

All in all, you should remember that the actual movements you make while playing or singing is the last step in a long and complex process of mental activity. Physically speaking, the only thing you can do to improve dexterity is maybe build up your finger muscles (or diaphragm for singers). Otherwise, the entire process is performed in the brain and nervous system. Therefore, following a routine of practice and improvement that is based on the mental process of musicianship will be far more effective than any other approach.

As mentioned before, nothing replaces practice. But the best technique for improving dexterity is to incorporate certain elements into a specialized practice routine and to perform a list of other exercises based on harnessing mind-power and optimizing how the nervous system works. Realize that one hour of effective practice that utilizes these techniques of mind power can equal 2 or 3 hours of ordinary practice. Discipline and hard work alone will not always guarantee tremendous results. But maximizing the power of the mind in addition to hard work will always achieve success.

10
Summary

THIS BOOK IS the product of four years of research and writing. I am by no means a professional writer. The perspective from which I have approached this project is that of a musician, and I truly believe that writing this book from a musician's point of view has made all the difference. Any research into the mental aspects of musical performance can only be truly applied if the author knows the needs, thoughts, and feelings of musicians.

The development of musical skill and the act of performing and creating music is definitely a unique combination of mental and physical effort. It is unlike any other art form or physical sport. It may be the ultimate example of the ability of the human nervous system to move muscles with precision and timing, equal to that of any athlete. If it were to end there, it would still be an impressive feat. Nevertheless, added to that mechanical skill is the ability for deep artistic expression (equal to that of any actor or artist), the requirement of intense learning and memory (if studied in depth, equal to that of any accountant or lawyer) and the ability to master one's nerves for a performance before an audience (equal to that of any lecturer).

Overall, the mental aspects of playing music certainly warrant special practice and development. In this book, we have learned how to improve a musician's learning and study habits. We've dealt with improving memory and concentration. Creativity and songwriting were addressed as were developing confidence and overcoming stage fright. Of course, we looked at strengthening motivation. All this was done by learning a little about neurological mechanics and applying that knowledge to musical skill, learning the exact methods and techniques for controlling the subconscious, and taking advantage of how the mind works.

I personally feel that the chapter on motivation is one of the most important, because once you become totally psyched and "catch the music bug" there is no stopping you. At that point, all the other information in this book is icing on the cake (although still very useful and can do wonders for your musical ability). But only by having the initial "bug" will you even bother to use any of what is taught in this book.

If you were to read the biographies of great musicians, the one thing they all have in common is that they were totally obsessed by music. They would play all day long. When they were away from their instruments, all they could think about was getting home and playing. Some psychologists may suggest that an obsession like this is emotionally unhealthy, but almost any great skill is first based on obsession. The world's great chess players are obsessed and play chess all day long. Olympic athletes will wake up at 4:00 in the morning to begin a daily routine of 12 to 14 hours of practice. There definitely is such a thing as a healthy obsession, especially if you are working towards a goal of excellence.

If you can, try to re-read and highlight this book. You might want to read it the first time to gain an overall understanding of mind control and the various techniques, but it may be beneficial to read it a second time to organize the information into a planned approach.

One suggestion is to write notes and draw an outline of how you want to plan a specific program. For example, you might want to outline a plan to overcome stage fright. Within this book, I have tried to list many techniques and approaches to the aspects of musical development. You may feel it best to streamline the information concerning stage fright into a daily or weekly agenda of techniques. Although I have tried to categorize my information and techniques, you may find a more effective or more personalized arrangement that works better for you. However you want to utilize what is taught in this book, the most important point I want to make is this; change takes time and effort. Techniques that directly affect the subconscious will require continued effort before you will see results. Many of the methods I've set forth in this book can take effect very fast and save years of work, but you still have to be disciplined in using these techniques in order to see consistent results. Don't be led to believe that after one week of creative visualization, self-hypnosis, and positive thinking habits, you will suddenly be able to totally overcome stage fright, write masterpiece songs, or concentrate with razor sharp focus. You have to be willing to commit to these methods for a few weeks to see real results and consequently a few months to see absolute change. You will not see beneficial results with just an occasional session every few weeks or months. You will need a concentrated effort. And once you feel satisfied with the results, it would still be wise to continue your efforts as a means of maintaining your improvements. Nothing in life is given to you for free, but the techniques found in this book will reduce the price from years down to months.

Also, I would recommend doing some additional reading on some of the various subjects on which I have based my techniques. An example is meditation. As you have seen, I stress the point that meditation is a super multipurpose musical skill improvement technique and will do wonders for dexterity, focus, creativity, confidence and just about any other aspect of musical skill and performance. Because of the neurological benefits to the nervous system, brain and thought process, meditation is probably the best thing a musician can do for him/herself with the exception of practice. Considering how valuable this one exercise is it may behoove you to do your own research into this field. I feel there is always more you can get out of a subject if you read multiple books about it. With today's Internet, a musician now has another valuable resource for information. If time is tight, be confident that this book does a thorough job of combining these various subjects into an effective approach for improving musical skill. If you do have extra time, additional reading is a good idea. I have confidence that if you really apply the information that I've presented, you will reap great results. Applying knowledge with effort and focus can achieve great things. At the very least a musician will be more aware of how the brain, nervous system, and sub-conscious affects the playing and creation of music. It is my definite belief that the reader of this book will be able to use this knowledge to greatly improve all aspects of musical performance and creation.

About The Author

Doug Oliver has been a musician, composer, and music teacher for over twenty years. He records and produces original music from his home recording studio and is currently working on his second CD. "Mind Power for Musicians" was started in 1999 and is the result of over four years of research and study.

9 781594 576645